AFRICOM AT 5 YEARS:
THE MATURATION OF A
NEW U.S. COMBATANT COMMAND

We must start from the simple premise that Africa's future is up to Africans. . . . We welcome the steps that are being taken by organizations like the African Union. [At the same time,] when there's a genocide in Darfur or terrorists in Somalia, these are not simply African problems—they are global security challenges, and they demand a global response. . . . And let me be clear: Our Africa Command is focused not on establishing a foothold in the continent, but on confronting these common challenges to advance the security of the America, Africa, and the world.

> Remarks by U.S. President Barack Obama
> to Ghana's Parliament,
> July 11, 2009

INTRODUCTION

At the time of President Obama's 2009 Africa policy speech quoted above, the U.S. Africa Command (AFRICOM) had existed as a combatant command for less than 2 years, and had come under sharp criticism since its inception, both in Africa and the United States. In this context, Obama felt compelled as Commander-in-Chief to affirm before an African audience his strong support for AFRICOM's mission of promoting greater security in Africa. Three years later, as AFRICOM passed the milestone of its 5th anniversary, and as a new U.S. administration enters 2013 in a period of far tighter budgets, it is timely to reflect on this Command's creation, its evolving role in the interagency process, its reception in Africa, and the way it might accomplish its mission in the future in a more cost-effective, policy-relevant way. To address these issues, this Letort Paper is divided into five parts.

Part I examines the posture of AFRICOM's headquarters and components, and the historical context leading to the Command's creation in 2007. Part II focuses on AFRICOM's unique interagency team and makes policy recommendations for new Goldwater-Nichols-type legislation to promote what this author calls new jointness in interagency cooperation. Part III answers the questions of whether AFRICOM has undermined the U.S. Department of State (DoS) interagency lead and militarized U.S. foreign policy, engaged in development work appropriately, and worked well in interagency coordination and strategic planning. Part IV examines the important issue of African attitudes toward AFRICOM, and analyzes three damaging, yet perennial, myths about AFRICOM involving Africa's energy resources, China's rise in Africa, and France's views of AFRICOM. Finally, Part V examines AFRICOM's future, including the significance of the Command's new allocated forces; whether the U.S. Government can ally more selectively with African democratic leaders; how AFRICOM could strengthen African regional approaches to security; where the Command's headquarters should be located; and why the threat of U.S. strategic insolvency means AFRICOM must right-size, including examining carefully its investments in intelligence assets.

Some readers may question the first part of this Paper's title, "AFRICOM at 5 Years," pointing out that the Command reached full operating capability only in October 2008 — i.e., less than 5 years ago. In AFRICOM's case, the milestone of 5 years is a useful literary hook, however, and AFRICOM *did* achieve initial operating capacity under the U.S. European Command in October 2007. Moreover, the lore of AFRI-COM's bureaucratic birth also suggests a 5-year mark. According to a senior George W. Bush administration U.S. Department of Defense (DoD) official responsible for Africa, AFRICOM was conceived in the summer of 2006, when then-Secretary of Defense Donald Rumsfield ordered a study of a future U.S. Africa Command over the strong objections of senior military officials in the U.S. European Command. Whatever the real background behind AFRICOM's creation, this Paper describes how the Command has grown and matured greatly since 2007 into an active, geographic combatant command responsible for an area of the world—the vast African continent—with some of the most important and challenging issues for U.S. national security.

PART I - AFRICOM: HISTORICAL CONTEXT OF ITS CREATION AND CURRENT POSTURE

U.S. Perceptions of Africa's Geostrategic Importance before AFRICOM's Creation.

Reflecting the end of World War II and the start-up of the Cold War, the two earliest, still existing, geographic combatant commands are the U.S. European Command and the U.S. Pacific Command, which were created in 1947.[1] The DoS established its Africa Bureau in 1958, signaling the importance that the United States placed on political relations with a growing number of independent African countries.[2] By contrast, the DoD cartography of Africa was dictated by Cold War geopolitics. During the Cold War, Africa remained a low military/security priority for the United States, despite the numerous proxy wars

Washington was tacitly or directly supporting on the continent.[345] Africa was not even included in the U.S. military command structure until 1952, when several North African countries were added to the European Command.[6] In 1983, responsibility for Africa was divided between the European, Central, and Pacific Commands[7]—a structure that persisted until AFRICOM's creation in 2007.

After the end of the Cold War, U.S. military policymakers saw little need to court African leaders.[8] DoD's 1995 U.S. Security Strategy for Sub-Saharan Africa, for example, concluded that "ultimately we see very little traditional strategic interest in Africa."[9] The 1998 bombings of U.S. Embassies in Nairobi, Kenya, and Dar Es Salaam, Tanzania, were an inflection point toward greater U.S. strategic interest in Africa. In 1999, DoD opened the African Center for Security Studies to support the development of U.S. strategic policy toward Africa—a move that could be seen as a precursor to its creation of AFRICOM in 2007.[10] DoD recognized that establishing a regional center dedicated to Africa made sense, given the continent's rising importance, but could not yet justify a much larger proposition—a geographic combatant command (CCMD) for Africa.

The terrorist attacks of September 11, 2001 (9/11), also marked a turning point in U.S. strategic policy toward Africa. The events of 9/11 forced a reassessment of and placed greater attention on the presence of extremists on the continent.[11] One result was the creation of the Combined Joint Task Force—Horn of Africa in 2002, ostensibly to capture Islamic fighters fleeing from Afghanistan and the Middle East. In 2003, an academic had called for the creation of "U.S. Forces Africa," but his proposal was not accepted by the U.S. Government.[12]

Around the mid-2000s, the U.S. Government reached a tipping point in its views of Africa's significance. For example, in its March 2006 U.S. *National Security Strategy*, the Bush administration concluded that "Africa [held] growing geostrategic importance and [had become] a high priority."[13] In congressional testimony that same month, Commander General John P. Abizaid of Central Command stated that he viewed the Horn of Africa as "vulnerable to penetration by regional extremist groups, terrorist activity, and ethnic violence." General James L. Jones of the European Command pointed out in 2006 that his Command's staff was spending more than half its time on African issues, up from almost no time 3 years earlier. That same year, General Bantz Craddock, Jones's successor, stated that Africa in recent years had posed "the greatest security stability challenge" to [the U.S. European Command] and "a separate command for Africa would provide better focus and increase synergy in support of U.S. policy and engagement."[14]

Consistent with the advice of General Craddock, President Bush decided in 2007 to create AFRICOM.[15] AFRICOM's creation also marked the disappearance of the one of the U.S. Government's last organizational vestiges of the colonial period and Cold War in that U.S.-Africa security relations were no longer subordinated to the European Command.

In a November 21, 2012, speech at Chatham House in London, United Kingdom (UK), AFRICOM Commander General Carter Ham made informal comments that reflected the above timeline:

Africa, to be completely honest, is not a part of the world that the United States military has focused on very intently until recently. We have had previously only a very small number of U.S. military intelligence analysts who focused on Africa and an extraordinary but small community of attachés with repetitive assignments and experiences on the African continent.... That changed in the mid-2000s. And I think amidst military engagement in other parts of the world, there was a growing recognition in the United States that Africa was increasingly important to the United States in a number of areas, certainly economically but politically and diplomatically as well from a development standpoint and also from a security standpoint. So in the mid-2000s there was a decision to establish the United States military command that was exclusively focused on the African continent.[16]

Factors Leading to and Shaping AFRICOM's Creation in 2007.

In the above section, we presented a historical timeline leading to AFRICOM's creation. While useful, this timeline lacks a deeper explanation of the historical context and intellectual changes that were also important to AFRICOM's creation, shaping, and core raison d'être. In this section, the author argues that in the 1990s and 2000s, there were two kinds of changes—geostrategic and operational—that explain *why* AFRICOM was created, and another kind of change—intellectual—that shaped *how* it was created:

Geostrategic.

The two major geostrategic factors behind AFRICOM's creation in 2007 were:

1. The Rise of Nonstate Actors in Africa: Terrorists and Criminals. Of primary importance was the rise in the 1990s in Africa of two kinds of nonstate actors: Violent Extremist Organizations and illicit traffickers. Box 1 below presents background on the rise in the 1990s of three terrorist organizations in Africa. By the mid-2000s, African countries were also facing asymmetric threats from well-funded criminal cartels — for which there is also an increasing nexus with terrorist organizations — engaged in illicit trafficking in drugs, arms, counterfeit goods, people, endangered animals; piracy; oil theft; illegal fishing, and illegal dumping of waste on land and at sea. One striking example was the emergence starting in 2005 of large-scale cocaine trafficking through West Africa to Europe carried out by the same Latin American cartels who sold their drugs in North America.

We argued above that the more important of two major geostrategic factors behind AFRICOM's creation in 2007 was the rise of two nonstate actors: terrorists and criminals. For background, we discuss here three examples of emerging terrorism threats in Africa that existed at the time of AFRICOM's founding to make a case that the geostrategic threat of terrorism was a valid justification for AFRICOM's creation in 2007 (and arguably an even stronger case for the Command's continued existence today):[17]

1. Al-Qaeda's Links to Africa, U.S. Embassy Bombings. Al-Qaeda was formed in August 1988 by several leaders of the Egyptian Islamic Jihad, who agreed to join with Saudi Arabia national Osama bin Laden in their fight against the Soviet invasion of Afghanistan. After condemning the Saudi government for its alliance with the United States following Iraqi dictator Saddam Hussein's 1990 invasion of Kuwait, Riyadh forced bin Laden into exile in Sudan from 1991 to 1996.

**Box 1. Three Major Terrorism Groupings
in Africa Starting in the 1990s.**

In 1996, the U.S. DoS accused Sudan of being a "sponsor of international terrorism," and bin Laden himself of operating "terrorist training camps in the Sudanese desert." Even though bin Laden left for Afghanistan later that year under pressure from the United States and Saudi Arabia, he had already aided al-Qaeda-trained terrorists and affiliates to set up shop in other parts of Africa.[18] For example, al-Qaeda-affiliated operatives were behind the 1998 bombings of the U.S. embassies in Kenya and Tanzania.

2. Al-Qaeda in the Islamic Maghreb (AQIM). This al-Qaeda affiliate was known until 2007 as the Salafist Group for Preaching and Combat. The group began in 1997 as a splinter faction of the Armed Islamic Group, which itself had fought a bloody insurgency against the Algerian military government with the help of Algerian mujahedeen fighters returning from Afghanistan. The group came to prominence in 2003 with the spectacular kidnapping of 32 European tourists, using a kidnap-for-ransom tactic that the group has since used repeatedly to generate large revenues for operations. Although this al-Qaeda affiliate has its origins in Algeria and was co-founded by Algerian jihadists returning from Afghanistan, it now poses a serious threat to multiple countries in the Sahel, from Mauritania to Mali, Niger, and Chad.[19] In March 2012, the group took over the northern half of Mali with Touareg allies in the chaos following a coup d'état. The group has become particularly dangerous since reportedly acquiring surface-to-air missiles during the chaos following the fall of Libya's Muammar Qaddafi, from whose regime it also recruited mercenary soldiers as new jihadist fighters.

3. Al-Shabaab in Somalia. According to a November 2012 Africa Center for Strategic Studies brief, "*Islamic militancy in Somalia first surfaced in the mid-1980s with the formation of al Itihad al Islamia ("Islamic Unity"), which expanded it military operations in the early 1990s.*"[20]

**Box 1. Three Major Terrorism Groupings
in Africa Starting in the 1990s. (cont.)**

Al Itihad seemed to disappear after 1996, but influenced the Islamic Courts Union (ICU) that emerged in the mid-2000s. In 2006, in the months leading up to AFRICOM's founding, Ethiopian forces invaded Somalia and defeated the ICU, which had taken control of parts of Somalia.[21] The ICU's military wing splintered off that year and launched an insurgency under the name of al-Shabaab.[22] It eventually gained control of most of the southern part of Somalia, where it imposed its own strict form of Sharia law.

In February 2012, al-Shabaab officially pledged loyalty to al-Qaeda.[23] (It was already considered by the United States to be an al-Qaeda affiliate, and had been designated in 2008 as a foreign terrorist organization.) Al-Shabaab controlled the majority of Somali territory until the summer and fall of 2012, when fighters of the African Union Mission in Somalia (AMISOM), backed by Ethiopian and Kenya forces, drove it out of Mogadishu, Kismayo, and largely into the bush. Prior to this, al-Shabaab had attacked ships and ransomed their crews as a way to finance its operations. This created a piracy crisis in the entire Horn of Africa down to the Mozambique Channel—an area that would have overlapped the old areas of responsibility of the European, Central, and Pacific Commands.[24]

Box 1. Three Major Terrorism Groupings in Africa Starting in the 1990s. (cont.)

2. Africa's Growing Economic Importance. Of secondary importance to terrorist concerns was Africa's growing economic importance in the world, both as a source of strategic natural resources, including oil, gas, and minerals, and increasingly as a market. By 2007, Angola and Nigeria had already become important suppliers of oil to the United States, and projections pointed toward the Gulf of Guinea region as a growing major source of U.S. energy imports.[25]

Today, it may seem obvious, ex post facto, that a separate U.S. geographic combatant command should have been created for Africa in recognition not only of the continent's growing strategic importance, but of its position straddling Europe, the Arabian Peninsula, and the global shipping lanes of East and West Africa, where piracy and illicit trafficking at sea have emerged as major problems. As AFRICOM's J-5 Director, Major General Charles Hooper, recently framed it:

> Djibouti, on the Horn of Africa, is a mere 20 miles across the Bab el-Mandeb waterway from Yemen and the Arabian Peninsula. Similarly, the eastern coastline of Africa is also the western shore of the Indian Ocean, sitting astride the sea lines of communication that link the continent and Europe to the rising powers of the Asia-Pacific region. In the north, Tunisia is less than 70 miles from Sicily, and only the Strait of Gibraltar separates Spain from Morocco . . . . [The] Gulf of Guinea [in West Africa is] a region important not only to Africa but increasingly to the United States as well.[26]

Operational.

There were also two important *operational* imperatives behind the creation of AFRICOM:

1. Existing Combatant Commands Were Overstretched, Distracted. The European and Central Commands had become overstretched by the mid-2000s, particularly given the wars in Iraq and Aghanistan. The European Command was primarily focused on relations with European allies and Russia, while the Pacific Command was primarily focused on China, India, and North Korea.[27] (As earlier comments by Generals Jones and Craddock suggest, the European Com-

mand also highlighted the ever-growing importance of its Africa engagement, in part to display continued relevance in the era of the Global War on Terror.)

2. Closing Seams. Crises in Africa had revealed "seams" between the Commands' boundaries that needed to be closed. For example, one seam was located between Sudan (then within the Central Command's area of responsibility), Chad, and the Central African Republic (then within the European Command's area of responsibility). This was an area of chronic instability with regard to the situation in Darfur and occasionally with regard to the Lord's Resistance Army. Another seam was caused by the fact that most countries in Africa were within the European Command's responsibility, but the headquarters of the African Union (AU) were in Addis Ababa, Ethiopia, which was within the Central Command's responsibility. (In this sense, AFRICOM can be viewed as an internal reorganization of DoD's combatant command structure to rationalize lines of authority.[28])

Intellectual Changes in Thinking about Geopolitics Shaped AFRICOM.

Beyond these geostrategic and operational reasons *why* AFRICOM was founded are four important intellectual changes in thinking about geopolitics in the 1990s and 2000s that also shaped *how* AFRICOM was created and structured. While AFRICOM was perceived externally by some as an act of military hubris internal to the U.S. defense community, it was deeply influenced by a sober realization of the limits of military capability without close coordination with other elements of national power. The following four intellectual changes were also key in how AFRICOM was created:

1. Intertwined Security and Development. After the end of the Cold War, donor states realized that if the security sector disregarded the rule of law, democratic principles, and sound management practices, sustainable, poverty-reducing development would be nearly impossible to achieve.[29] In Africa, security challenges are inextricably bound up with the challenges of development, and contributions to solve each are mutually reinforcing.[30]

2. Emphasis on Conflict Prevention/Stability Operations, Vice Conduct of War. In conventional U.S. military doctrine, there are four phases of a military campaign: 1) deter/engage; 2) seize initiative; 3) decisive operations; and, 4) transition.[31] While U.S. armed forces have traditionally focused on "fighting and winning wars," military thinkers introduced in the 1990s an additional phase, "Phase Zero (0)," which focuses on conflict *prevention* through increased emphasis on theater security cooperation and building the capacity of allies.[32] Similarly, another key lesson is that Phase 4, "transition" or "stability operations," may eclipse combat operations when determining victory.[33] Increasingly the ability of Africans to prevent, mitigate, and resolve conflicts leads to increases in stability and thus development.[34] In 2005, DoD recognized "stability operations" as a "core U.S. military mission" that ought to "be given priority comparable to combat operations."[35] (DoD also emphasized building the capacity of partner states in its *Quadrennial Defense Review*.)[36]

3. Human Security and the "Responsibility to Protect." Human security is a post-Cold War paradigm that has reshaped the traditional notion of national security by arguing that a people-centered view of security is necessary for national, regional, and global stability.[37] Responsibility to Protect is a corollary concept, endorsed by the United Nations (UN) in 2005,

based on the idea that sovereignty is not a right, but a responsibility. This concept focuses on the prevention of four mass atrocity crimes: genocide, war crimes, crimes against humanity, and ethnic cleansing.[38] The influence that Responsibility to Protect has had on AFRICOM is directly observable in the Commander's Intent statement in Box 2, where the Command's top military officer, General Ham, included a specific reference to the prevention of mass atrocities.[39]

As we consider AFRICOM's brief history and the context in which it was created, it is also useful to consider its current mission. In his November 2012 Chatham House talk cited above, General Ham also laid out AFRICOM's top five priorities in the context of overall U.S. defense strategy:

> A . . . document I suspect many of you have read is . . . the 2012 Defense Strategic Guidance . . . When the document was released, I had the opportunity to talk with many of my African counterparts, both military and civilian, and frankly they were concerned because when you read that document, you will see that the word "Africa" appears precisely one time. And so our African partners say—looked at that and say, does this mean that you no longer care about Africa?

> And I said . . . rather than think that the number of times the word appears is important, look at the tasks that are outlined in that document for the United States armed forces and see what you think about the relevance of Africa then. Unsurprisingly, at the top of the list for tasks for the United States armed forces is the defeat of al-Qaida, its associated networks and to prevent further attacks on America, Americans and American interests. That's not sur-

---

Box 2. AFRICOM's Mission and Commander's Intent.

prising to you. The sad fact is we do a lot of that work in Africa today. We want to work to a point where we don't have to do as much work. Secondly, there's a lot of discussion in the document about the necessity for continued strategic access to the global commons for economic growth, to allow free access globally to markets and for the global economy to continue to prosper. Certainly we do a lot of that work in Africa. A third priority is building—what we call building partner capacity [or] strengthening the defense capabilities of allied and partner nations, so that they can first of all deter conflict; so that the commitment of military forces, whether they be U.S. or other, is less and less likely. We think that's a high priority, and we certainly do that in Africa as well. An increasingly important priority for the United States military is the prevention and response to mass atrocity. Sadly, Africa has had this experience, and we work carefully with our African partners in that area as well. And lastly, the United States military is expected to be prepared to assist others with humanitarian assistance and disaster relief, wherever that may occur. And of course that's certainly work that is conducted in Africa as well.

AFRICOM's latest mission statement indicates how the Command puts U.S. national interests first, while also helping Africa. It also indirectly frames the issue of fighting violent extremist organizations and terrorism in terms of defeating "transnational threats" (which can also include illicit trafficking in drugs, stolen oil, arms, and people, as well as pandemic threats such as HIV/AIDS and avian influenza):

[AFRICOM] protects and defends the national security interests of the United States by strengthening the defense capabilities of African states and regional organizations and, when directed, conducts military operations, in order to deter

Box 2. AFRICOM's Mission and Commander's Intent. (cont.)

and defeat transnational threats and to provide a security environment conducive to good governance and development.[40]

Similarly, the Commander's Intent, which is typically a subordinated but more detailed and unclassified guidance to members of the Command, indicates that AFRICOM's activities, plans, and operations are centered on two guiding principles. These principles frame AFRICOM's activities not in terms of interfering with the internal affairs of African nations, but rather in working together to promote Africa's stability. Put differently, AFRICOM wishes to "lead from behind" and let African partners address their own security challenges with U.S. assistance:

> A safe, secure, and stable Africa is in our national interest. Over the long run, it will be Africans who will best be able to address African security challenges and that AFRICOM most effectively advances U.S. security interests through focused security engagement with our African partners.[41]

General Ham elaborated on his internal but unclassified guidance, Commander's Intent, in an August 2011 address to Command staff. His following elaboration of the Command's priorities speaks to both fighting terrorism as the most important geostrategic reason for AFRICOM's creation and to the issues of helping African nations promote democracy, peace and stability, and prevent mass atrocities (including genocide):

- Deter or defeat al-Qaeda and other violent extremist organizations operating in Africa and deny them safe haven.
    - Strengthen the defense capabilities of key African states and regional partners. Through enduring and tailored engagement, help them build defense institutions and military forces

Box 2. AFRICOM's Mission and Commander's Intent. (cont.)

that are capable, sustainable, subordinate to civilian authority, respectful of the rule of law, and committed to the well-being of their fellow citizens. Increase the capacity of key states to contribute to regional and international military activities aimed at preserving peace and combating transnational threats to security.

— Ensure U.S. access to and through Africa in support of global requirements.

— Be prepared, as part of a whole-of-government approach, to help protect Africans from mass atrocities. The most effective way in which we do this is through our sustained engagement with African militaries.

— When directed, provide military support to humanitarian assistance efforts.[42]

Box 2. AFRICOM's Mission and Commander's Intent. (cont.)

4. "New Jointness,""Whole of Government,"and "3D" Interagency Cooperation. Based in part on "lessons learned" slowly in the Balkans in the 1990s and repeated in Iraq and Afghanistan in the early-2000s, DoD embraced counterinsurgency strategies in the mid-2000s that recognized the need for a new jointness or whole-of-government approaches toward meeting national security objectives. DoD has also embraced a subset of new jointness or whole-of-government, known as the 3D approach to security. This approach recognizes the role of *diplomacy,* led by the DoS, and that of *development,* led by the U.S. Agency for International Development (USAID), alongside *defense* in predicting and preventing conflict. DoD issued *Joint Publication 3-08* in 2006 to provide guidance to facilitate coordination between the DoD and interagency

organizations.[43] The 2008 *U.S. National Defense Strategy* also stressed the military's commitment to these two new concepts.[44]

AFRICOM's Posture Today: Headquarters and Components.

What, exactly, is the U.S. AFRICOM? It is the newest of the six DoD geographic combatant commands.[45] Table 1 shows how these six combatant commands divide the globe into their respective areas of responsibility:

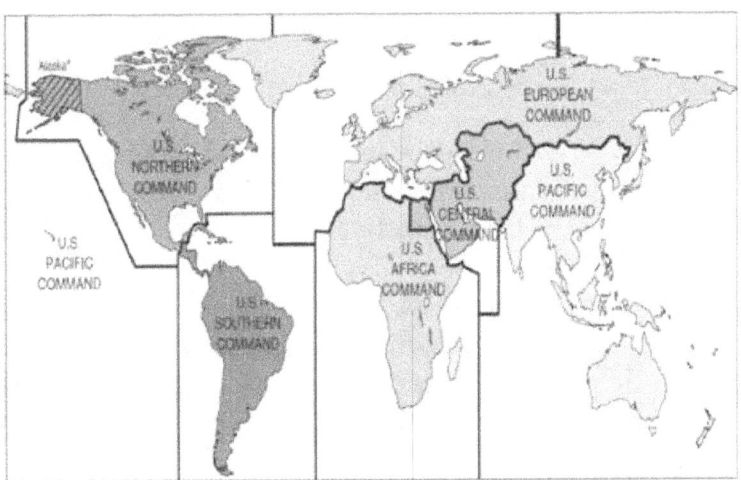

Source: U.S. Government Accountability Office (GAO) presentation of DoD data.

Table 1. U.S. Combatant Commands' Areas of Responsibilities as of October 1, 2008.

Table 2 shows the areas of responsibility and examples of activities transferred to AFRICOM in 2007 from these three other combatant commands.[46]

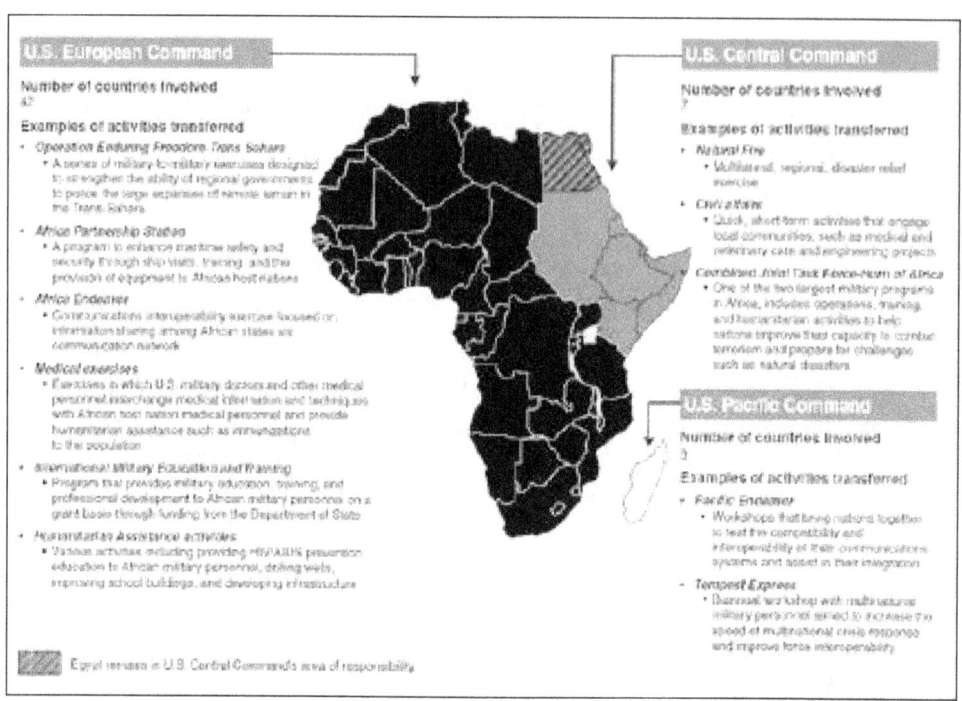

U.S. European Command

Number of countries involved
43

Examples of activities transferred

- *Operation Enduring Freedom-Trans Sahara*
  - A series of military-to-military exercises designed to strengthen the ability of regional governments to police the large expanses of remote terrain in the Trans-Sahara.

- *Africa Partnership Station*
  - A program to enhance maritime safety and security through ship visits, training, and the provision of equipment to African host nations.

- *Africa Endeavor*
  - Communications interoperability exercise focused on information sharing among African states and communication network.

- *Medical exercises*
  - Exercises in which U.S. military doctors and other medical personnel interchange medical information and techniques with African host nation medical personnel and provide humanitarian assistance such as immunizations to the population.

- *International Military Education and Training*
  - Program that provides military education, training, and professional development to African military personnel on a grant basis through funding from the Department of State.

- *Humanitarian Assistance activities*
  - Various activities including providing HIV/AIDS prevention education to African military personnel, drilling wells, improving school buildings, and developing infrastructure.

U.S. Central Command

Number of countries involved
1

Examples of activities transferred

- *Natural Fire*
  - Multilateral, regional, disaster relief exercise.

- *Civil affairs*
  - Quick, short-term activities that engage local communities, such as medical and veterinary care and engineering projects.

- *Combined Joint Task Force-Horn of Africa*
  - One of the two largest military programs in Africa; includes operations, training, and humanitarian activities to help nations improve their capacity to combat terrorism and prepare for challenges such as natural disasters.

U.S. Pacific Command

Number of countries involved
3

Examples of activities transferred

- *Pacific Endeavor*
  - Workshops that bring nations together to test the compatibility and interoperability of their communications systems and assist in their integration.

- *Tempest Express*
  - Biannual workshop with multinational military personnel aimed to increase the speed of multinational crisis response and improve force interoperability.

▨ Egypt remains in U.S. Central Command's area of responsibility.

Table 2. Areas of Responsibility and Examples of Activities Transferred to AFRICOM from Other Combatant Commands as of October 1, 2008.

As its name suggests, AFRICOM is responsible for all DoD operations, exercises, and security cooperation in 54 of 55 nations on the African continent, its island nations, and surrounding waters.[47] The single exception has been Egypt, which, because of that nation's strong ties to the rest of the Middle East, has remained part of the Central Command.[48] As of the end of fiscal year (FY) 2012, AFRICOM had approximately 2,300 assigned personnel, including U.S. military, civilian, and contractor employees. About 1,500 personnel work at the command's headquarters at Kelly Barracks in Stuttgart. Others are assigned to AFRICOM units at MacDill Air Force Base near Tampa, Florida, and the Joint Analysis Center in Molesworth, England. AFRICOM's service component commands and theater Special Operations Command component are:

- U.S. Army Africa: Operating from Vicenza, Italy, it conducts sustained security engagements with African land forces to promote security, stability, and peace. 1,600 personnel.[49]
- U.S. Naval Forces Africa: Headquartered in Naples, Italy, its primary mission is to improve the maritime security capability and capacity of African partners. Personnel are shared with U.S. Naval Forces Europe. 900 personnel.
- U.S. Air Force Africa: Based at Ramstein Air Force Base, Germany, it conducts sustained security engagement and operations to promote air safety, security, and development in Africa. 954 personnel.
- U.S. Marine Corps Forces Africa: Located in Stuttgart, it conducts operations, exercises, training, and security cooperation activities throughout the African continent. Staff is shared with the U.S. Marine Corps Forces Europe. 319 personnel.
- Special Operations Command Africa: A theater Special Operations Command component, Special Operations Command Africa is co-located at AFRICOM's headquarters in Stuttgart. 600 personnel.
- Combined Joint Task Force-Horn of Africa: Located at Camp Lemonnier, a Forward Operating Site in Djibouti with approximately 2,000 personnel (400 staff and 1,600 forces).[50] Camp Lemonnier can also be considered AFRICOM's only base on the African continent.[51]

AFRICOM's other forward operating site besides Combined Joint Task Force—Horn of Africa is on UK's Ascension Island in the south Atlantic. It also has Cooperative Security Locations in Algeria, Botswana, Gabon, Ghana, Kenya, Mali, Namibia, Sao Tome and Principe, Sierra Leone, Tunisia, Uganda, and Zambia.[52] The location of AFRICOM, its service components, and its theater Special Operations Command component are shown in Table 3.

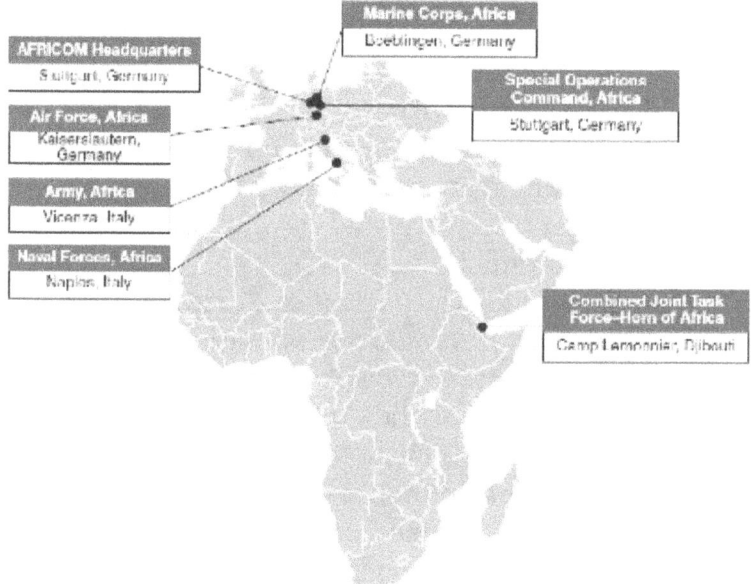

Table 3. Locations of AFRICOM Headquarters and Its Components.

AFRICOM estimates that the U.S. military footprint on the continent (exclusive of Egypt) averaged approximately 3,500 troops in 2010. This includes the personnel at Combined Joint Task Force-Horn of Africa and the rotational presence of forces participating in various exercises, such as the annual communications interoperability exercise African Endeavor; operations such as JUNIPER SHIELD;[53] theater security cooperation activities such as the Navy's Africa Partnership Station; and various conferences and meetings.[54]

PART II - AFRICOM AND THE NEW JOINTNESS OF INTERAGENCY COOPERATION

The fourth intellectual change noted above that affected *how* AFRICOM was formed — the growing need for new jointness or whole-of-government in interagency cooperation — is also a useful segue into a discussion of the *interagency* team at AFRICOM compared to two other geographic combatant commands — the Southern and Pacific Commands.[55] AFRICOM has commonly been referred to as a "CCMD Plus," because it has all the roles and responsibilities of a traditional geographic combatant command, but also a: 1) broader "soft power" mandate aimed at building a stable security environment; and, 2) a relatively larger contingent of personnel from other U.S. government agencies, including a civilian Deputy Commander for Civil-Military Affairs to carry out this soft power mandate.[56]

While AFRICOM may be the first combatant command to be labeled as a CCMD Plus, in recent years all geographic combatant commands have been placing increased emphasis on soft power and improved interagency coordination. The way AFRICOM has gone about it, however, has been unique. Before AFRICOM's creation in 2007, DoD officials testified that, to better synchronize military efforts with other U.S. Government agencies, they intended that AFRICOM's headquarters be staffed three-quarters from DoD civilians and military, and one-quarter from other U.S. Government agencies.[57] However, despite DoD's good intentions, budget realities at other agencies and a lack of available personnel kept AFRICOM from coming even close to achieving this initial vision.[58] At its peak in 2011, the Command had only 38 interagency representatives—less than 2 percent of headquarters staff, and less than one-tenth of the original 25 percent goal.

After a dramatic lowering of its initial expectations, AFRICOM currently has a new goal of 53 interagency positions within the command structure beyond those—such as Foreign Policy Advisors—traditionally assigned to combatant commands.[59] This would imply interagency staffing of roughly 3 percent. Given the extremely tight budgetary climate expected for FY2013 and beyond, however, even this new goal is unlikely to be attained under AFRICOM's current Memoranda of Understanding with other agencies, which have been reluctant to send more personnel to AFRICOM. Some, including the Treasury Department, have even looked seriously about cutting back on their existing personnel in Stuttgart.[60] Indeed, AFRICOM's interagency staffing numbers are likely to fall in the future unless the Command agrees to cost-sharing with partner agencies, particularly for embedded personnel. In this regard, it would be useful, should Congress take up new Goldwater-Nichols-type legislation to promote new jointness, that any new law specifically include guidance or principles for cost sharing between combatant commands and other agencies for salary, cost of living, housing, and moving expenses.[61]

Interagency Team within AFRICOM.

Aside from the Deputy to the Commander for Civil-Military Activities and the Foreign Policy Advisor, the DoS augments the AFRICOM headquarters with 11 other personnel spread between the:

- J-3 (Operations), where a Foreign Service Specialist from the Bureau of Diplomatic Security works;[62]
- J-5 (Strategy, Plans, and Program), where seven Foreign Service Officers (FSOs), including a senior (FS-1 or O-6 equivalent) advisor to the J-5 Director, sit in the J-5 front office.[63] In addition, there is one action officer each in the five Regional Engagement Branches (North, East, South, Central, and West), and a planner in the Plans sub-directorate. There is also one civil servant representative of State's new Bureau of Conflict and Stabilization Operations;[64]
- J-9 (Outreach), which is headed by a Senior FSO and also has two other FSOs, at least one of whom has experience in public diplomacy in Africa.[65]

Additionally, each of AFRICOM's six component commands, including Combined Joint Task Force-Horn of Africa as well as Special Operations Command-Africa, has a Foreign Service Officer serving as a Foreign Policy Advisor, typically at the FS-1 (O-6 or Colonel-equivalent) level.

Broadly speaking, all State Foreign Service Officer positions at AFRICOM are managed by the DoS Political-Military Bureau, through its Political Advisor program. This important program is building a cadre of FSOs who can bridge the bureaucratic cultural gap between diplomacy and defense, but it has faced a number of serious challenges.[66] First, there are significantly fewer FSOs available than Political Advisor positions. Second, incumbents of Political Advisor positions have historically had fewer promotion opportunities, particularly into the FS-1 and OC ranks (O-6 and O-7 equivalents), where supervision of ever larger numbers of personnel is practically a prerequisite.

If Congress were to consider Goldwater-Nichols legislation for the interagency, it should make officers take at least one interagency excursion tour during a career as a requirement for promotion into the senior ranks.[67] For State, this might mean requiring an interagency detail before promotion into the "senior" ranks, defined here as FS-1, or before promotion into the Senior Foreign Service.[68] While the current DoS promotion precepts instruct promotion boards to give credit for interagency service, these precepts also ask boards to weigh many other factors in deciding on whom to recommend for promotion. The net effect is that interagency service in most cases is a net negative for career advancement, not a positive.

The other U.S. agency at AFRICOM representing one of the 3Ds is USAID, which has three staff members in Stuttgart. The Senior Development Advisor reports directly to the Commander;[69] a senior USAID official heads the J-5 Health and Humanitarian Action Branch; and a representative of the Agency's Office of Foreign Disaster Assistance is in the combined J3/J4.

In terms of interagency players apart from DoS and USAID, AFRICOM currently has a small contingency of over 20 personnel from more than 11 other U.S. Government departments and agencies, including Agriculture (J-5), Energy (J-5), Commerce (J-9), Justice/FBI (J-5), Homeland Security Investigations (J-5), Transportation Security Administration (J-5), the Coast Guard (J3/J4, J5, J9), and the intelligence community (J-2), including the Office of the Director for National Intelligence and National Security Agency.[70] A few of these interagency representatives act solely as liaison officers, but most are embedded into AFRICOM.[71]

Aside from the percentage of interagency representatives at its headquarters, two other issues AFRICOM faced during its initial standup were how interagency representatives should be distributed within the Command's organizational structure, and whether interagency representatives should be pure liaison officers or embedded. As noted above, AFRICOM has chosen to spread out interagency representatives among several of its directorates.[72] By contrast, the U.S. Southern Command has interagency players concentrated at its Joint Interagency Task Force-South, the latter focusing on an anti-narcotics mission.[73] The U.S. Pacific Command, for its part, has tended to group interagency players in the J-9 outreach branch—an approach that has been criticized by some as isolating the interagency from other directorates, while praised by others as an efficient way for Command teammates in a large combatant command to have a one-stop shop for interagency advice and coordination.

The spreading of interagency representatives at AFRICOM into different directorates does not currently pose problems with ease of access, vice concentrating them in the J-9. One important reason was that the AFRICOM Foreign Policy Advisor started monthly Interagency Forum meetings, which allowed interagency representatives in different Directorates to get to know each other and noninteragency teammates.[74] This Forum, currently chaired by the J-9 Director and an elected member of the interagency, was created in the wake of a 2008 Government Accountability Office (GAO) report that found that the Command needed to take new steps to improve the integration of its interagency representatives.[75] At these Forum meetings, invited speakers present views on various issues of importance to the Command, as well as discuss the professional, personal, and family challenges of work and life in Stuttgart. The Forum also regularly shares electronically, throughout the Command, contact information for members of the Interagency—thereby creating a virtual one-stop interagency presence and making it unnecessary to have a common directorate (e.g., as was the case for the J-9 at Pacific Command).

The author's view is that AFRICOM's approach was more appropriate for AFRICOM in that most mid-level interagency players in Stuttgart acted both as liaison officers to their home agencies *and* as embeds, whose day-to-day work contributed directly to ongoing Command operations. At AFRICOM, the reality for most interagency representatives was that there was not enough work to justify a full-time liaison officer, and therefore being embedded in an appropriate Directorate, e.g., Treasury in the J-5, made the most sense. Of course, the reality is that every Command is different and no one size fits all. For example, some observers have praised Southern Command for having a mature interagency planning process—a situation that had not been the case at AFRICOM and will be discussed further below. Southern Command has also identified members of its interagency to be the lead for each of its Theater Security Objectives,[76] a best practice that AFRICOM should follow to further the early involvement of interagency partners. The amount of interagency work at Pacific Command, which is many times larger than AFRICOM, may also justify more pure interagency liaison positions and a centralization of interagency teammates into its J-9.

Accepting interagency teammates at its headquarters and components has not been the entirety of AFRICOM's commitment to the whole-of-government approach. AFRICOM has also significantly expanded the number of DoD personnel who are integrated into U.S. embassies across Africa over the past 3 years. Along with DoD personnel detailed to other agencies in locations within the United States, this is the new jointness flip side of AFRICOM's receiving interagency representatives at its headquarters and components. Some of these new DoD personnel are Defense Attachés, who typically come from the Defense Intelligence Agency (DIA). Most of the new personnel, however, are placed in new or existing Offices of Security Cooperation, typically led by Army, Navy, or Air Force Foreign Area Officers, with emerging Africa expertise and a rank of Lieutenant Colonel or Colonel (O-5 or O-6). These personnel, and the enlisted staff who support them, are valuable members of U.S. Embassy country teams and interact daily with their fellow Embassy colleagues from State, USAID, and other agencies.

Should Other Combatant Commands Upgrade the Role of the Senior Interagency Representative?

The most distinctive CCMD Plus feature at AFRICOM has been the appointment of a DoS Senior FSO as the Deputy to the Commander for Civil-Military Activities and one of two co-equal Deputy

Commanders along with the Deputy Commander for Military Operations, a three-star Lieutenant General or Vice Admiral. [77] The Deputy to the Commander for Civil-Military Activities has broad responsibilities and directs the command's plans and programs associated with health, humanitarian assistance and de-mining action, disaster response, security sector reform, and Peace Support Operations. He or she also directs Outreach (J-9), strategic communications, and AFRICOM's partner-building functions, as well as assures that policy development and implementation are consistent with U.S. foreign policy.[78] The three incumbents of AFRICOM's Deputy to the Commander for Civil-Military Activities position have all been former Ambassadors with personal ranks of Minister-Counselor (two-star equivalent).[79] All three also brought to the Command deep geographic expertise on Africa that simply did not exist previously within AFRICOM or its predecessor components within the U.S. European Command.[80]

At the U.S. Southern Command, by contrast, the senior DoS representative has been dual-hatted as Civilian Deputy to the Commander and Foreign Policy Advisor. This senior DoS representative has primary responsible for overseeing the development and ongoing refinement of the Command's regional strategy and strategic communications, but has more narrow responsibilities.[81] At the U.S. Pacific Command, the senior DoS representative has an even more limited role as an advisor and is not presented on the Command's website as part of its leadership, but rather appears as one of about 20 members of the Commander's "Special Staff," in the "J-0."[82]

If one accepts the premise that cross-fertilization within the U.S. Government to achieve a new jointness can be significantly advanced by accepting more detailees from other agencies, it also follows that giving senior leaders from other agencies more substantive, supervisory responsibilities in one's own agency is a desirable new step. Given the increased emphasis in the U.S. foreign policy community in recent years on soft power activities and whole-of-government approaches, the author believes other geographic combatant commands should consider whether a dual civilian-military Deputy Commander or some lesser but yet upgraded role for their top interagency representative would also be desirable. For Southern Command, this might mean: 1) upgrading the position of Deputy to the Commander to a co-equal Deputy Commander, as at AFRICOM; and, 2) creating a separate position for a Political Advisor or Foreign Policy Advisor to travel with and advise the Commander. For the Pacific, Central, and European Commands, this could mean upgrading the Foreign Policy Advisor into a Deputy to the Commander, as at Southern Command, where the senior State officer is considered to be part of the Command's top leadership and has much more than just an advisory role. It would also be desirable that the appropriate role of the top interagency representative at each combatant command be considered by Congress should it decide to pursue Goldwater-Nichols-type legislation on new jointness.

PART III - INTERNAL PERCEPTIONS OF AFRICOM: ROLE IN FOREIGN POLICY, DEVELOPMENT WORK, INTERAGENCY COORDINATION, AND STRATEGIC PLANNING

As noted above, the creation of AFRICOM in 2007 was controversial, both in the United States and abroad. This section addresses four criticisms that have been made of AFRICOM from within the U.S. Government, analyzes whether they are true, and describes how the Command has responded to them. These four criticisms are that the Command: 1) has undermined the DoS's interagency lead and militarized U.S. foreign policy; 2) has gotten "out of its lane" by doing development work and doing it badly; 3) is a poor interagency teammate; and, 4) does not adequately integrate its strategic planning with the rest of the U.S. Government.

1. Has AFRICOM Undermined the DoS Interagency Lead and Militarized U.S. Foreign Policy? Broadly addressing the issue of "mission creep" by DoD into areas that have traditionally been the prerogative of the DoS, the U.S. Senate Foreign Affairs Committee found in 2006 that:

> As a result of inadequate funding for civilian programs . . . . U.S. defense agencies are increasingly being granted authority and funding to fill perceived gaps. Such bleeding of civilian responsibilities overseas from civilian to military agencies risks weakening the Secretary of State's primacy in setting the agenda for U.S. relations with foreign countries and the Secretary of Defense's focus on war fighting.[83]

Supporting this view, Defense Secretary Gates stated in November 2007 that:

> We must focus our energies beyond the guns and steel of the military. We must focus our energies on the other elements of national power that will be so crucial in the years to come. . . . What is clear for me is that there is a need for a dramatic increase in spending on the civilian instruments of national security.[84]

In the same speech, Secretary Gates compared the yearly defense appropriation—at the time about $500 billion, not counting the war in Iraq and Afghanistan—with an annual DoS budget of $36 billion. He noted that even with new hires, there were 6,600 career U.S. diplomats, or "less than the manning of on aircraft carrier strike group" (and about the size of a Brigade Combat Team).[85]

Consistent with this, and specifically referring to Africa, one Capitol Hill source told the author that Congress has:

> increasingly granted the Department of Defense its own foreign military assistance authorities (Section 1206, including a new provision for anti-Lord's Resistance Army support, and a new Section 1207 for East Africa so [that] AFRICOM does . . . increasingly have its own tools with which to engage African countries.[86]

Additionally, a comparison of summer 2011 staffing levels between 1) AFRICOM, 2) the entire DoS as a whole, and 3) DoS's Africa Bureau, while a case of comparing an apple and two oranges, is nonetheless indicative of the disparity in human resources between the U.S. military and the lead civilian agency responsible for national security/foreign policy for Africa:

- AFRICOM staffing levels—assuming 2,000 personnel in Stuttgart, Molesworth, and Tampa,
  and 3,200 in Djibouti—added with the staffing
  at AFRICOM's component commands, total
  approximately 9,000 personnel.
- DoS *worldwide* staffing levels of American personnel, by contrast, were as follows: 11,500
  from the diplomatic corps (6,500 FSOs and
  5,000 Foreign Service specialists (security, medical, finance, communications, secretarial), and
  8,000 from the civil service.[87]
- DoS *Africa Bureau* staffing was only about 200,
  of whom about 150 were FSOs and civil servant
  desk officers, and about 50 were administrative
  and clerical support staff.[88]

Does the above mean that AFRICOM has undermined the DoS interagency lead and militarized U.S.
foreign policy? The author believes that the answer is
a clear "no." The fact that AFRICOM is well funded
does not in itself mean that it has "taken over" the DoS
interagency lead. In reality, AFRICOM is not a leader
in making U.S. national security/foreign policy for
Africa, but rather a primary *implementer* of this policy.
Several of the initiatives that AFRICOM implements
are actually foreign military assistance programs carried out under the direction and funding of the DoS to
promote democracy and the rule of law and to prevent
pandemic diseases.[89] For example, AFRICOM, in support of the DoS Global Peace Operations Initiatives
and Africa Contingency Operations and Training and
Assistance Program, provides military mentors to
support pre-deployment training to support African
nations which provide forces to AMISOM and other
peacekeeping operations.[90] Additionally, as noted in

the discussion in Box 3 of AFRICOM's mission and programs, Operation JUNIPER SHIELD is carried out in support of the DoS Trans-Sahara Counter-Terrorism Partnership, and the HIV/AIDS in the military program promotes goals of the DoS Office of the Global AIDS Coordinator.

AFRICOM carries out its Theater Security Cooperation programs in support of AFRICOM's top five mission goals. The *2012 Strategic Guidance* recognizes that building partnership capacity "remains important for sharing the costs and responsibilities of global leadership" with states that value "freedom, stability, and prosperity." AFRICOM's theater strategy has, since its inception, built its foundation on two principles:

1. A safe, secure, and stable Africa is in the U.S. national interest; and,

2. Over the long run, it will be Africans who will best be able to address African security challenges, and AFRICOM most effectively advances U.S. security interests through focused security engagement with African partners.

AFRICOM's J-5 Director has explained the Command's focus on capacity building as follows:

Some may argue that changes in the strategic environment diminish the value of building partner capacity as a component of our nation's overall defense strategy. It makes more sense, they say, to dedicate those scarce resources toward improving our own capability than to improve those of other partners. We disagree. Building the capacity of our . . . partners is not a strategic indulgence but rather an ensuring strategic imperative. . . . A prominent example of how building the security capacity of our African partners promotes the sharing of costs and responsi-

**Box 3: Security Cooperation—
The Cornerstone of AFRICOM's Engagement.**

bilities, supports our national interests, and provides a high return on modest investments is our sustained support to the African Union Mission in Somalia. . . . Our direct and indirect efforts . . . contribute to an African Union organization increasingly capable of securing ungoverned space, defeating al-Shabaab, and creating the conditions for a functioning state of Somalia.

Following are a few of AFRICOM's programs and activities that help the Command meet these mission goals via three primary capacity building functions: building operational capacity, building institutional capacity, and developing human capital:

1. Building Operational Capacity.

a. Operation JUNIPER SHIELD, formerly known as Operation ENDURING FREEDOM – TRANS-SA-HEL (OEF-TS), is DoD's supporting effort to the DoS Trans-Sahara Counter-Terrorism Partnership program, which focuses on overall security rather than solely on counterterrorism. This program includes 10 African countries: Algeria, Burkina Faso, Chad, Mali, Mauritania, Morocco, Niger, Nigeria, Senegal, and Tunisia. Operation JUNIPER SHIELD trains and equips company-sized partner nation forces to help deter the flow of illicit arms, goods, and people, and also fosters collaboration and communication among participating countries.

b. Africa Partnership Station, the Command's premier maritime security engagement program, began in fall 2007 and is carried out by its Naval Forces-Africa component. As a multinational security cooperation initiative, this partnership helps strengthen Africa's maritime security capacity through maritime training, collaboration, infrastructure building, and cross-border cooperation. The partnership focuses on addressing four primary focus areas: maritime pro-

Box 3: Security Cooperation –
The Cornerstone of AFRICOM's Engagement.
(cont.)

fessionals, maritime infrastructure, maritime domain awareness, and maritime response capability. Expertise shared during the mission includes law at sea, port security, maritime interdiction operations, small-boat maintenance, medical training, and more. In 2010, the partnership included representatives from 9 European allies, 17 African countries, and Brazil. Its aim is to improve maritime safety and security in Africa, while building lasting relationships. Africa Partnership Station in 2011 consisted of seven U.S. ships and conducted activities with 22 African nations whose exchanges involved more than 7,000 maritime professionals. Several African navies are now planning jointly, sharing information at sea, and working together as a result of this partnership. This includes multinational exercises off the west and east coasts of Africa as well as in the Gulf of Guinea.

      c. AFRICOM also carries out a number of other programs such as exercises designed to strengthen the operational capacity of African militaries, including Exercise Flintlock, Exercise Natural Fire, Exercise MEDFLAG, and a State Partnership Program under which the National Guards of several U.S. states are partnered bilaterally with individual African nations, such as the Michigan National Guard with Liberia.

    2. Building Institutional Capacity.
      a. In January 2010, AFRICOM began a 5-year defense sector reform program, Operation ONWARD LIBERTY, to support the DoS's broader security sector reform program in Liberia. The program provides 50-60 uniformed U.S. military mentors and advisors, primarily from Marine Forces Africa, to the Armed Forces of Liberia. Liberia also reactivated its Coast Guard in February 2010, and, under the defense sector reform program, the U.S. Coast Guard provides

Box 3: Security Cooperation—
The Cornerstone of AFRICOM's Engagement.
(cont.)

a senior officer as a maritime advisor and to oversee funding and training.

b. AFRICOM established the Africa Maritime Law Enforcement Partnership program in 2008 to help African nations counter illicit activities, including illegal oil bunkering, poaching of fisheries, drug trafficking, and piracy. The program, through bilateral maritime law enforcement agreements, shares with partner nations the Coast Guard's law enforcement skill set for conducting law enforcement boardings, gathering evidence, maintaining chains of custody, and, at sea, space accountability. Coast Guard Law Enforcement Detachments are embarked aboard U.S. Navy or Coast Guard vessels, where they train African partners and actually engage with them in law enforcement operations.

c. Other AFRICOM programs designed to address institutional capacity are Exercise Africa Endeavor, the Partnership for Integrated Logistics Operations and Tactics, and the Pandemic Response Program.

3. Developing Human Capital.

a. AFRICOM helps to professionalize militaries and reinforce the democratic value of elected civilian authority though funding from the DoS-led International Military Education Training programs and an enhanced version of this program known as E-IMET. These programs are the most widely used military assistance programs in AFRICOM's area of responsibility and have contributed to stronger bilateral military relationships between the United States and partner countries. Regional seminars with a U.S. Defense Institute for International Legal Studies military education teams funded by this program have helped many nations implement security sector and judicial sector reform. Many African officers and enlisted graduates

**Box 3: Security Cooperation—
The Cornerstone of AFRICOM's Engagement.
(cont.)**

of this program go on to fill key positions in their militaries and governments.

    b. AFRICOM's HIV/AIDS in the Military program reaches 40 African countries and is aimed at mitigating the impacts of the disease on African military readiness and assisting in the development and implementation of culturally focused, military-specific HIV prevention, care, and treatment programs. AFRICOM implements this program on behalf of the DoD's HIV/AIDS Prevention Program Office and the State Department Office of the U.S. Global AIDS Coordinator in support of the President's Emergency Plan for AIDS Relief.

Box 3: Security Cooperation —
The Cornerstone of AFRICOM's Engagement.
(cont.)

AFRICOM's J-5 Director recently used budgetary figures and authorities to make the point that AFRICOM plays only a *"supporting* (emphasis added) role to broader U.S. Government efforts across Africa" and demonstrates this support through Command's "close collaboration with the State Department as well as other agencies":

> Military engagements comprise a small but critical element of U.S. Government activities in Africa. To illustrate this, compare the Department of State and USAFRICOM spending in Africa. In fiscal year 2012 (FY 12), the Department of State spent approximately $7 billion on the . . . countries in our [area of responsibility] on a wide array of health, development, and security programs under its Title 22 authorities. Approximately $3.3 billion of this $7 billion funded security-related programs such as peacekeeping, nonproliferation, antiterrorism, narcotics control and law enforcement, military education, and equipment financing. . . . By

contrast, USAFRICOM in FY 12 controlled, influenced, and administered a modest $515 million in Title 22 and Title 10 security cooperation program dollars. . . . USAFRICOM then supported and administered $130 million in traditional Department of State Title 22-funded programs such as Foreign Military Financing, International Military Education and Training . . . . [Africa Contingency Operations Training and Assistance] . . . the Partnership for Regional East Africa Counterterrorism, . . . [Trans-Sahara Counter Terrorism Partnership] . . . and [the] Africa Maritime Security Initiative.[91]

2. Has AFRICOM Done Development Work Badly? A second U.S. Government internal criticism of AFRICOM, and a subset of the first criticism that AFRICOM is taking over the DoS lead in U.S. national security/foreign policy, is that the Command is: carrying out development work when it should not; and, 2) doing so badly. In terms of 1), these critics believe the United States should restrict the activities of its military personnel to training and equipping programs, and instead implement all development projects through USAID, nongovernmental organizations (NGOs), international organizations, and private development firms.[92] Beyond AFRICOM "getting out of its (bureaucratic) lane," officials at USAID have also been concerned that humanitarian and development projects could be "stigmatized" by links to the military,[93] waste taxpayers' money,[94] and do more harm than good in the recipient countries, thereby undermining U.S. national security/foreign policy. These observers complain that AFRICOM's development activities are largely ad hoc, without a plan to support lasting change, and without regard for a broader development strategy.[95]

What to make of these critics? AFRICOM *can* be fairly criticized for the execution of some of its development projects, but these criticisms appear to be overblown for two reasons. First, it is actually senior DoS and USAID officials in Stuttgart—not military officers—who are responsible for oversight and implementation of the development projects at AFRICOM. AFRICOM's Deputy to the Command for Civil-Military Activities has been given formal oversight for all development-related projects at the Command. The head of the Humanitarian Affairs Branch within AFRICOM's J-5 has always been a senior USAID Foreign Service Officer who reported to this Deputy Commander through the J-5 Director and Deputy Director for Programs.[96]

Second, the actual amounts of funding for AFRICOM's "development" projects are quite small, and these projects usually have a clear link to security/military affairs.[97] DoD, for example, established an HIV/AIDS prevention program with African armed forces.[98] Of the $150 million dollars in FY2011 that AFRICOM spent on development and health-related activities, 87 percent was actually HIV/AIDS-related. Since the rate of infection in some African militaries is high, reportedly as high as 50 percent in some southern African countries, this is an important public health as well as military-related program. Given that African militaries prefer mil-to-mil engagements instead of working with donor-country development agencies, it is appropriate that AFRICOM currently provides oversight to this program via USAID staff detailed to the Command.

After subtracting out this HIV/AIDS in the military program, the Command had less than $20 million in "humanitarian assistance"—a modest amount that belies the notion that AFRICOM is militarizing

U.S. aid to Africa. By contrast, USAID's Africa bureau alone programmed more than \$4.1 billion in development assistance for FY2011 — excluding food aid and emergency response programs.[99]

This is not to say that there have not been serious problems with some AFRICOM-led development projects. For example, an April 2010 GAO report criticized Combined Joint Task Force-Horn of Africa's management of humanitarian and development projects.[100] GAO found that AFRICOM lacked procedures for tracking and following up on the Task Force's development projects, and for ensuring these projects appropriately fit within broader U.S. foreign policy goals. For example, the GAO visited a dilapidated school that the Task Force had built but long forgotten, and a well that the Task Force had dug without considering how the placement could cause conflicts within clan relationships. The GAO linked part of this mismanagement to the Task Force's extremely short tour rotations and insufficient cultural sensitivity training — the net result of which was to undermine the attempts at wielding soft power in the region.[101] As another example, research by Tufts University's Feinstein International Center found similar dysfunction in the Task Force's "hearts and minds" activities in eastern Kenya.[102] Kenyan recipients were grateful for a successful development project, but much more likely to maintain an opinion of the U.S. military informed by its operations in Iraq and Afghanistan.[103]

Since Djibouti is the host country for AFRICOM's only forward-operating site on the continent, the author believes that it makes sense for the Command to sponsor civilian action projects in Djibouti itself, relative to other countries in the Horn of Africa. Nevertheless, even in the case of Djibouti, these projects should not be led by military personnel, other than policy guidance from AFRICOM in Stuttgart and civil-military affairs officers in Djibouti, but rather by USAID in conjunction with the local Embassy country team. For the rest of Horn of Africa countries, it would be preferable to let embassy country teams lead in project selection as part of the Mission's Strategic Resources Planning strategy. They should do this while working in a collaborative fashion with the Senior Defense Official at Post, shaping the projects so that they also meet their Theater Security Objectives.[104] In this regard, it is notable that DoD's creation of Senior Defense Officials at Embassies—the Defense Attaché or Chief of the Office of Security Cooperation—has helped to relieve some of the confusion at embassies about how the various DoD components in a given country report to the Ambassador.

3. Poor Interagency Coordination? AFRICOM Improves Greatly. A third internal U.S. Government criticism of AFRICOM is that the Command has not coordinated well with the rest of the interagency. In the author's view, this may be the criticism with the least validity because AFRICOM has rightly been cited as a unique organization that has been an "experiment" or even "model" for whole-of-government approaches. Nevertheless, some observers, including the GAO, have found that AFRICOM was not living up to expectations regarding integration of its work with the rest of the foreign policy community.[105] These observers have asserted that this outcome is not surprising, because U.S. national security and foreign policy institutions have long been stovepiped from one another with their own priorities and "alien" bureaucratic cultures. Drawing from a well-known book analyzing

the differences between men and women, some have used the metaphor that DoD personnel are from Mars, while DoS and USAID staff are from Venus.[106]

At the end of the day, are these criticisms fair? To do its job well, AFRICOM needs to address three levels of interagency coordination:

1. Coordination with U.S. Embassies in Africa, which are headed by Ambassadors constitutionally appointed by the President, and whose country team members also typically include representatives from multiple agencies;[107]

2. Coordination between the Command in Stuttgart and U.S. Government agencies in Washington;[108] and,

3. Internal coordination with the Command between military officers and DoD civilians on the one hand, and non-DoD interagency civilians on the other.

The author's research for this Paper and prior professional experience while at AFRICOM suggest that, early on in its existence, AFRICOM *did* have at least limited problems with all three types of interagency coordination, but that—by and large—AFRICOM *overcame* these issues as the Command matured:

a. AFRICOM's Coordination with U.S. Ambassadors and their Missions. With regard to AFRICOM's relations with U.S. embassies, good interagency coordination requires respect by the Command of Chief of Mission authority, both from a policy and operational perspective. Theresa Whelan, then Deputy Assistant Secretary of Defense for African Affairs, stressed in early 2007 that European Command had established good working relationships with U.S. Ambassadors and expected that AFRICOM would do so as well:

The creation of U.S. Africa Command [will] not in any way subordinate U.S. Ambassadors to the Command, or the DOD, or put the Command in any position to be able to dictate to those Ambassadors what they will or will not do. The command, just like European Command today, Central Command today, and Pacific Command today . . . will continue to be a supporting effort to those Ambassadors in regards to peacetime mi-to-mil relations with the countries in which those Ambassadors serve.[109]

For AFRICOM, starting in 2007, there was also some degree of internal chaos as the young Command staffed up at a rapid rate and developed new internal procedures. With only some exaggeration, "veterans" of the transfer from the European Command have described to the author how the Command grew from a core of little more than a dozen staffers in 2007 to over 2,000 in a little over 4 years—an extraordinary rate of growth that would have challenged the best leaders and managers.[110] The author believes that fumbles with the interagency and U.S. embassies during the early years with AFRICOM likely had less to do with a "military takeover" and bad faith than with a lack of clear internal procedures to ensure good coordination.[111]

Consistent with this benign interpretation of AFRICOM's initial coordination problems, a DoS Office of Inspector General report of August 2009 assessing the capacity of the Department's Africa Bureau found problems with internal communication within the DoS, not AFRICOM:

Inadequate communication between the Bureau and embassies led to confusion about AFRICOM's role and the parameters of U.S. ambassador's authority in the beginning, although the [Office of the Inspector General] found that 'there is every indication that the new Assistant Secretary and the AFRICOM Commander are working cooperatively'. [112]

AFRICOM's Commanders have also actively courted U.S. Ambassadors during Command briefs to visiting Chief of Missions passing through Stuttgart and during trips by the Commanders on the continent. Most Ambassadors pass through the Command on their way to post, or wait 6 months to get their feet on the ground before they come to the Command to discuss security cooperation and other AFRICOM activities in their host countries. After establishing this face-to-face contact, many Ambassadors have actively engaged with the Command's leadership, usually via the Commander, but also sometimes directly with the heads of Directorates such as the J-2, J-5, and J-9. Over time, U.S. Ambassadors have learned to appreciate the additional resources that AFRICOM can bring to their diplomatic missions.

If there has been any continuing friction between AFRICOM and U.S. Ambassadors, it has been largely operational in nature and due to the large numbers of AFRICOM temporary duty personnel deploying to the continent — and the significant logistical challenges they bring for smaller U.S. Missions with limited staff. AFRICOM's large and growing programming in Africa, while welcome, risks at times overwhelming the soft power of USAID and State programs and personnel, a senior DoS Africa Bureau official testified in 2011. [113]

Part of AFRICOM's improved interagency coordination with the rest of the U.S. Government and U.S. Embassies comes from effective communication of the Command's philosophy by its top leadership. General

Ham, for example, emphasized strong interagency coordination in remarks to his staff in 2011:

> Accomplishing our mission . . . requires us to ensure our military efforts are synchronized with many other in the U.S. Government. In some cases, Africa Command will be in the lead; in others, ours will be a supporting effort to another department or agency. Our military activities will always be in support of U.S. Government foreign policy and fully coordinated with affected U.S. Chiefs of Mission.[114]

AFRICOM's coordination with Ambassadors' staffs at the working level has also improved. For example, AFRICOM also engages in limited public diplomacy projects with a security theme. Because they involve outreach to host-nation publics, however, these projects should have U.S. Embassy approval and be implemented in coordination with the Embassy's Public Affairs Officer (PAO). In one West African country that the author visited in 2011, AFRICOM coordinated an outreach program to the Muslim community with the PAO. AFRICOM personnel reported directly to the PAO on their day-to-day work, with the result that both AFRICOM and the U.S. Embassy were pleased with the project outcomes.

b. AFRICOM's Coordination with the Washington Interagency. By all accounts, there have been strong *senior-level* working relationships between AFRICOM Commanders Ward and Ham and between Assistant Secretary of State for African Affairs Jendayi Frazier under the Bush administration and Ambassador Johnnie Carson under the Obama administration. Aiding strong AFRICOM-State high-level communication have been the Command's successive Deputy to the

Commander for Civil-Military Activities and Foreign Policy Advisors, who were also from the DoS.

While some observers have asserted that all-powerful Combatant Commanders can appear like rogue Roman pro-consuls engaging in foreign policy formulation, the reality could not be further from the truth at AFRICOM.[115] For example, Generals William Ward and Ham were entrusted by the DoS leadership with carrying certain security-related foreign policy messages to their military counterparts. Assistant Secretary Carson, for example, asked General Ward to pass a message to the interim President in Guinea, General Sekouba Konate, urging Konate to support the Presidential elections. This eventually contributed to the first democratic elections in that country's entire history.[116] Also, in innumerable meetings with Africa military and civilian leaders, including a great number of heads of state, both Commanders were effective diplomat-soldiers and symbolic "Ambassadors" for the United States in their own right.[117]

Indeed, AFRICOM has recently received praise for its work, not criticism from high-level State colleagues. In terms of AFRICOM's work with the interagency in Washington, State's Principal Deputy Assistant Secretary for Africa, Ambassador Donald Yamamoto, in July 2011 congressional testimony, praised AFRICOM's role in *"supporting"* (emphasis added) U.S. foreign policy on a broad range of issues:

> The U.S. Department of State has coordinated and collaborated with AFRICOM as it worked to achieve the Administration's highest priority goals related to democracy, good governance, the peaceful resolution of conflicts, and transnational challenges . . . AFRICOM has played an important *supporting* role in implementing this framework . . . . [Areas of coordination and collaboration include] military professionalization;

building counterterrorism capacity; disaster management; peacekeeping capacity building; humanitarian
operations coordinated with USAID; demining and
ammunition handling training; nonproliferation of
weapons of mass destruction; destruction of excess
small arms and light weapons and unstable ammunition; reduction of excess and poorly secured man-por-
table air defense systems. . . . Defense Sector Reform in
Liberia, [the Democratic Republic of the Congo], and
South Sudan; counter-piracy activities off the Somali
coast; maritime safety and security capacity building;
and civil-military cooperation.[118]

Ambassador Donald Yamamoto further noted
that AFRICOM elements at U.S. embassies implement DoS-funded Foreign Military Financing and
International Military Education and Training programs, which further U.S. interests in Africa by helping to professionalize African militaries and to train
and equip them toward common security goals.[119] In
other words, and as noted above, AFRICOM has been
supporting the DoS lead in foreign affairs by acting
as the *implementing* agency for certain programs for
which State retains the policy lead and the budget
purse strings.

Several other examples suggest that AFRICOM's
relations with the interagency at the *working level* are
also strong:

Counterterrorism: While at AFRICOM, the author
observed regularly scheduled, periodic, working-
level meetings between the DoS Africa Bureau staff
and mid-level AFRICOM personnel to support State's
Trans-Sahara Counter-Terrorism Partnership through
AFRICOM's implementation of Operation JUNIPER
SHIELD.[120] These meetings, which included the occasional participation of the J-3 Director and Deputy
Director for Operations, attested to the close and

professional working relationship between State and AFRICOM.

Counternarcotics: AFRICOM's Counternarcotics Office has been coordinating closely with the Drug Enforcement Administration (DEA), the Federal Bureau of Investigation (FBI), the Department of Homeland Security (DHS), U.S. Customs and Border Protection, and Treasury in West Africa, funding training activities and supporting maritime and airport interdiction efforts.[121]

Maritime Security: There has been excellent collaboration between AFRICOM's J-5 Air/Maritime Branch, the Africa Center for Strategic Studies, the DoS (Bureaus of African Affairs and Political Military Affairs and the Office of the Legal Advisor), the U.S. Coast Guard, and the U.S. Department of Justice to promote greater maritime security cooperation between the Economic Community of West African States, the Economic Community of Central African States, and their 25 member-states.

Law Enforcement: AFRICOM has worked well with State's Africa and International Narcotics and Law Enforcement Bureaus and on workshops with the Economic Community of West African States that are part of a trans-Atlantic maritime criminal justice program, and with the U.S. Coast Guard on the African Maritime Law Enforcement Program.

c. Internal Integration of Interagency Personnel at AFRICOM. A third part of AFRICOM's relationship with the interagency has been the integration of non-DoD civilians into the Command itself. A July 2010 GAO report indicated that:

AFRICOM has made efforts to integrate interagency personnel into its command and collaborate with other federal agencies on activities, but [was] not fully engaging interagency partners in planning processes.[122]

At the time that the author arrived at AFRICOM for a 1-year tour in July 2010, the GAO's assessment was accurate: most interagency colleagues wanted to be helpful, but at times felt excluded from certain Command work deemed inherently "military" in nature by uniformed and civilian DoD colleagues—the latter of whom were mainly retired military.

Interagency integration within AFRICOM progressed over time as representatives of various agencies became more familiar with the Command and its military bureaucratic culture and, as noted above, were aided by monthly Forum meetings chaired by the Foreign Policy Advisor. As discussed below, a systematic effort was made by the J-5 in early-2011 to seek interagency comments on its engagement plans and country work plans. The Command also started a fusion center in 2011 in the J-3 to support all of the Directorates; this center provides access to interagency staff assigned to help support it.

The watershed event for interagency integration at AFRICOM, however, was Operation ODYSSEY DAWN against Libyan dictator Muammar Qaddafi. After this operation was initiated, an interagency coordination cell was established to coordinate requests for information directed at the interagency. Several members of the interagency distinguished themselves during this period, notably U.S. Treasury officials addressing financial sanctions issues and the Department of Energy liaison officer, whose own knowledge and sources in Washington were crucial in understanding the damaged state of Libyan oil infrastructure. The star teammate, however, was the USAID Office of Foreign Disaster Assistance representative, who provided valuable insights into how the Command needed to work with the international donor community, e.g., to carry out repatriations of Egyptians fleeing into Tunisia from Libya. While AFRICOM's command and control during the operation could have been better,[123] and while the interagency had its own "lessons learned" from the operation, most non-DoD representatives felt immense pride at having been a small part of a military operation that garnered global attention, and a greater sense that they were now bona fide members of the AFRICOM team. In a broader sense, AFRICOM's success in the operation was also helpful in validating the Command's new jointness whole-of-government model because timely responses to certain requests for information would have been difficult, if not impossible, without inter-agency representatives present in Stuttgart.

Five years after AFRICOM's creation, overall inter-agency integration into the Command is now largely complete. While interagency individuals new to the Command still have to overcome initial bureaucratic "culture shock" of adapting to a military environment, the procedures and training to welcome them to the Command are in place, and their integration more rapid and complete.[124] This is not to imply, however, that all is perfect. There are some U.S. agencies that continue to question the valued of sending embedded officials to AFRICOM—a situation that could be improved if, as advocated above, the Command reached cost-sharing agreements more attractive to the agencies concerned.

d. AFRICOM Corrects the Interagency Strategic Planning Disconnect. A fourth area where AFRICOM received U.S. Government internal criticism but has subsequently matured and strengthened its integration into the foreign policy community is in strategic planning. AFRICOM completed its theater strategy and theater campaign plans in September 2008 and May 2009, respectively, with input from the DoS/ USAID Joint Strategic Plan, DoS Africa Bureau Strategic Plan, and USAID's Strategic Plan for Africa.[125] Table 4 shows the nesting of DoD planning documents starting from the U.S. National Security Strategy and National Security Presidential Directive 50 down to country work plans and their interaction with Embassy Mission Strategic Resource Plans (MSRPs).[126]

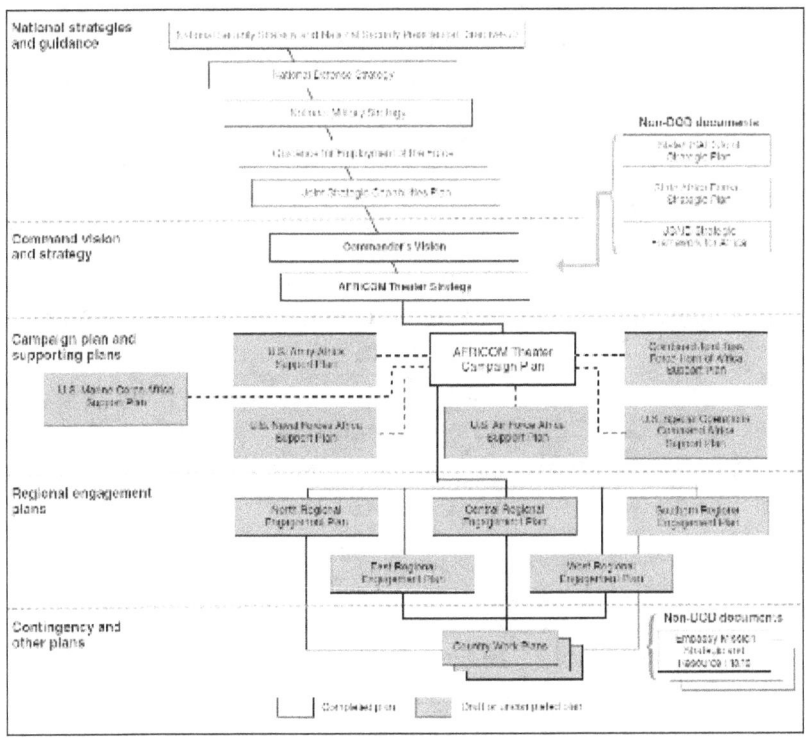

Source: GAO Presentation of DoD data.

Table 4. AFRICOM Strategic Plans, including Nesting with Non-DoD MSRPs.

AFRICOM had sought interagency input into its plans. The command invited interagency members from both Washington and U.S. Embassies in Africa to attend AFRICOM's annual Theater Security Cooperation Conference. Deputy Chiefs of Mission, who typically play a leading role with other country team members in crafting their Ambassadors' MSRPs, were particularly invited. However, as noted in a July 2010 GAO report, AFRICOM had not completed many of its supporting plans roughly 3 years after the Command's establishment. The Command's regional engagement plans were first drafted only in late-2010.The Command's work plans for the top 20-odd priority countries were being completed for the first time late in 2011 and early in 2012, with country work plans for lower-priority countries to be added in spring 2012—well over 4 years after the Command was established.[127] One unfortunate result of this was that the Command spent tens of millions of dollars of taxpayer money on training and equipment programs from 2007-2011, without detailed country-level strategic plans, without continuous consultation with officials from other agencies such as DoS and USAID, and without a truly effective assessments process with credible parameters to measure effects.

Fortunately, AFRICOM improved considerably in response to the 2010 GAO critique. The Command now has four "Subordinate Campaign Plans," which are hybrid thematic *and* geographic, and which include Intermediate Military Objectives that are measurable and achievable within 5 years. The four Subordinate Campaign Plans, as shown in Table 5, are organized geographically (and thematically) for:

- East (focused on counterterrorism, including related Somali piracy);

- North-West (focused on counterterrorism);
- Gulf of Guinea (focused on maritime security, and including all 25 member-states of the Economic Communities of Central and West Africa); and,
- Central (focused on the situation in the Democratic Republic of the Congo, as well as the Lord's Resistance Army problem).

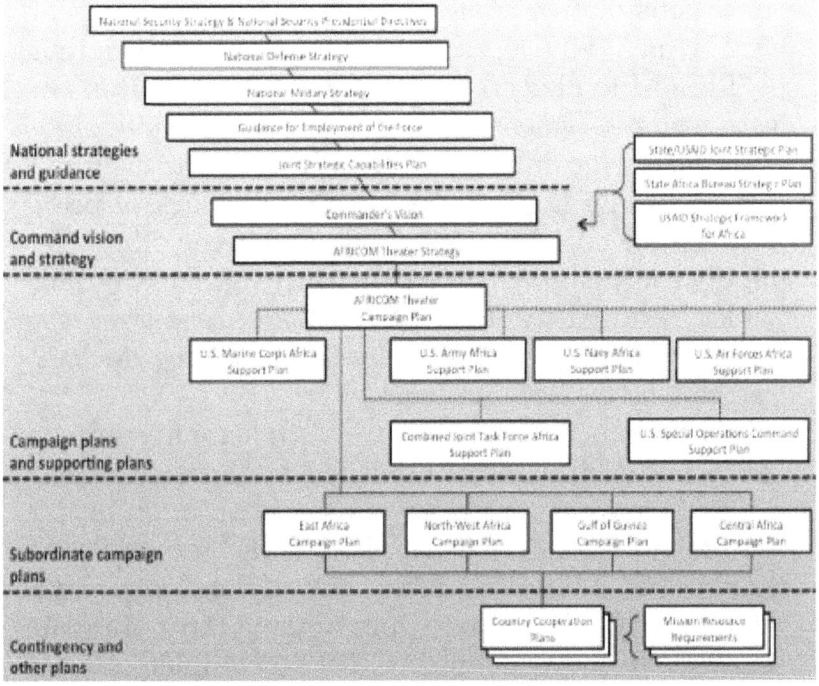

Table 5. AFRICOM Theater Campaign Plan, Component Plans, and Subordinate Campaign Plans.

The Subordinate Campaign Plan replaced five Regional Engagement Plans, which had covered all training, exercises and all other engagement activities for east, north, west, central, and southern Africa. A senior AFRICOM J-5 official acknowledged that the four new, more thematically focused Subordinate Campaign Plans did not cover southern Africa, and that the Command was willing to "take a modest amount of risk" in this regard.

AFRICOM has also improved its annual planning cycle. In the past, AFRICOM had been criticized by several federal agency officials" for having a single, large consultative conference at the end of the fiscal year, which only served to validate the criticism that AFRICOM tended to *plan activities first and then engage partners, rather than including interagency perspectives during the initial planning efforts."* One example cited by GAO of the problems that this lack of prior interagency coordination caused was in the otherwise highly successful Africa Partnership Station program, which resulted in *"unnecessary delays, confusion, and turmoil with the U.S. embassy in Ghana, during the 2009 port visit by the USS Nashville."*[128]

At the time of the GAO study's release in summer 2010, two critical but unfinished linkages in AFRICOM's planning process were the integration of the Command's country work plans with Embassy Mission Strategic Resource Plans, and of the Command's regional plans to the State Department's Africa Bureau Strategic Resource Plan. AFRICOM completed these linkages when it kicked off its new Annual Planning Cycle in 2011. The annual cycle begins with Country Cooperation Meetings in which the Command jointly develops Country Level Objectives with Chiefs of Mission and Host Nation officials. The objectives shape the Command's priorities prior to entering the latter half of the fiscal year, when a series of functional conferences are conducted that also support the development of the Subordinate Campaign Plans. The annual planning cycle concludes with the new AF-RICOM Theater Synchronization Conference in early September, to which are invited the State Department Assistant Secretary for African Affairs, the senior US-AID official for Africa, and Deputy Chiefs of Mission. Instead of being organized purely by region, this annual conference is organized based on each Subordinate Campaign Plan which, as noted above, is a hybrid plan focused thematically but also covering a discrete geographic areas.

Beyond improving its annual planning cycle, AF-RICOM has taken two other steps that have improved coordination with the Interagency:

1. AFRICOM, since its inception, systematically opened new Office of Security Cooperation offices — increasing from eight to almost three dozen. With the support of the DIA, AFRICOM has also added new Defense Attaches in a small number of new countries, including Burkina Faso. These new DoD teammates at U.S. Embassies in Africa, in daily contact with their interagency colleagues and with a much better on-the-ground appreciation of realities in their host government and country, have also helped interagency coordination.

2. AFRICOM's J-5 further established a small "Synchronization Division" to ensure proper coordination with U.S. Embassies and Washington, and has asked its planning teams to offer to brief U.S. Embassy front offices, particularly Deputy Chiefs of Mission, when visiting their host countries.[129]

PART IV - EXTERNAL PERCEPTIONS OF AFRICOM: AFRICA, ENERGY, CHINA, AND FRANCE

In this section, the author first addresses the critical issue of African attitudes toward AFRICOM and then debunks three damaging yet perennial myths about the Command's role in energy security, the rise of China in Africa, and France's alleged opposition to AFRICOM.

African Attitudes toward AFRICOM: Past, Present, and Future.

The number one theme for Sub-Saharan Africa in the *2012-13 Key Strategic Issues List* published by the Strategic Studies Institute (SSI) of the U.S. Army War College is "Assess the evolving role and organization of AFRICOM, *and its receptivity within Africa*" (italics added). SSI's focus on African reactions to AFRICOM is on the mark. So vociferous was initial African opposition to AFRICOM's creation in 2007 that the AU issued a nonbinding resolution asking member-states not to host AFRICOM on the continent. For its part, the Southern African Development Community, one of the AU's most important Regional Economic Communities, declared that none of its 14 member-states would be willing to host U.S. forces. Nigeria, Africa's most populous country and a regional powerhouse in West Africa, endeavored to block AFRICOM from establishing its headquarters in the Gulf of Guinea region.[130]

Pointing to 9/11, and U.S.-led wars in Iraq and Afghanistan, many African opinion leaders were concerned in 2007 that AFRICOM's founding reflected a growing militarization of U.S. relations with their continent and a new focus on anti-terrorism at the expense of traditional development aid.[131] They feared that — far from alleviating the continent's insecurity — AFRICOM would incite, not deter, terrorist attacks.[132] Some feared U.S. support for repressive regimes. Others accused the United States of a "new imperialism," and said AFRICOM was a tool for U.S. "exploitation" of Africa's oil and mineral wealth. Many African governments and civil society opinion leaders were also vehemently opposed to the creation of AFRICOM because:

- They felt inadequately consulted during the conceptualization of AFRICOM, and resented the Command as yet another *fait accompli* hoisted on the continent by a superpower not interested in listening to African views about their own future;

- AFRICOM's headquarters were originally proposed to be in Africa — a decision that revealed DoD's lack of understanding of the politics of the continent. Any country hosting a new U.S. military command, for example, would be severely criticized for violating Africa's common positions on African defense and security, which discourage the hosting of foreign troops on African soil;[133]

- Africans often have a very negative view of their own militaries because of past misbehavior, including coups, mistreatment of civilians, and corruption. Even though the reality is that U.S. military personnel are professional and committed to civilian control, they are perceived by some Africans as untrustworthy as African militaries or, even worse, as neo-colonialists;

- AFRICOM was particularly strongly opposed, at least initially, by countries such as South Africa and Nigeria, which saw it as a threat to their status as regional hegemons.
- There was also a concern that AFRICOM, even if initially a positive, "new" kind of CCMD Plus, would suffer from mission creep and evolve from an engagement and training focus to an interventionist force, such as allegedly occurred with Operation RESTORE HOPE in Somalia in 1992.[134]

Reacting to this vociferous African pushback, the Bush administration decided in May 2008 to defer any final decision on the location of AFRICOM's head-quarters. This resulted in more African states publicly acknowledging their willingness to work with the new Command, including Nigeria. By October 2008, the majority of African states had at least acquiesced to the idea that the U.S. military had established a military command responsible for Africa.[135] The GAO reported in February 2009 that DoD had also taken steps to clarify AFRICOM's mission, including publishing an approved mission statement, but had not yet finalized a strategy for future communication with African and other stakeholders.[136]

Since the 2009 GAO report, AFRICOM's leadership has used a more consistent and comprehensive communications strategy with African stakeholders. The Command's first head, General Ward, repeatedly emphasized in public that AFRICOM was a *"listening and learning"* organization. As a charismatic and outgoing African-American, General Ward was particularly effective in connecting with African military counterparts and the African public. AFRICOM's second Commander, General Ham, also strove to keep a consistent, positive narrative in public statements about the Command's mission. General Ham has often repeated in testimony and public comments the African proverb, "If you want to go quickly, go alone. If you want to go far, go together," adding in February 2012, for example, that:

> We, at US Africa Command, choose to go far. We choose to go together, with our African partners as well as together with our many interagency partners, to better meet their security interests and to advance the security interest of the United States.[137]

Beyond style, African governments and citizens have also seen for themselves, through AFRICOM's various engagement activities since 2007, that the new institution was not what they feared it to be, but instead was a continuation and sometimes expansion of existing U.S.-Africa security cooperation.[138] Consequently, AFRICOM has over time been received with cautious optimism by several African governments and militaries. They view increased American attention to the continent's problems as a positive development, potentially bringing increased resources, training, and assistance.[139]

In a farewell interview in September 2012 before leaving AFRICOM, then Deputy to the Commander for Civil-Military Activities Ambassador J. Anthony Holmes stated that a primary area where he had seen considerable progress was in the Command's relationship with African partners:

> The relationship that this Command has developed with African militaries over the four years since it was

formally stood up are so much more solid today. . . .
The level of suspicion one encounters is just a small
shadow of what it was four years ago.[140]

Consistent with this, current Deputy Assistant
Secretary of Defense for African Affairs, Amanda J.
Dory, stated in an October 2012 interview that:

> The U.S. military effort on the continent is being ac-
> cepted by many African leaders . . . when U.S. Africa
> Command first stood up, there was concern among
> some leaders that it signified a 'militarization of U.S.
> foreign policy and a sort of creeping colonialism'.
> Those fears have subsided.[141]

While AFRICOM's vocal opponents are becoming
fewer and perhaps more fringe than mainstream, the
Command cannot become complacent because there
remains strong opposition to AFRICOM among certain African audiences. Box 4 provides what is admittedly an unscientific sample of titles of articles that
appeared during a September 2012 Google search for
the keyword "AFRICOM." There are a broad range
of provocative articles opposing the Command with
titles such as: "AFRICOM's Imperial Agenda Marches
On," "Beware the Rotten Fruit of AFRICOM Training,"
"Resist AFRICOM—Puppet Masters," "AFRICOM or
Africon?" and "AFRICOM: Devil in the Backyard."[142]

Resist AFRICOM (1, N/A)
ASRP The Campaign to Resist AFRICOM (4, N/A)
AFRICOM's Imperial Agenda Marches On:
Black Agenda Report (9, 2012)
Beware the Rotten Fruit of AFRICOM Training
(12, 2012)
Globalist Warlord Obama Moves to Expand AFRICOM
Reach (12, 2011)
AFRICOM: Washington's New Imperial Weapon
(12, N/A)
Gaddafi vs AFRICOM and the Re-colonization of Africa
(13, 2012)
AFRICOM: Wrong for Liberia, Disastrous for Africa
(13, 2007)
Land Destroyer: Nigeria: The Next Front for AFRICOM
(13, 2012)
AFRICOM: A Wolf in Sheep's Clothing (16, 2011)
NATO, AFRICOM and the New White Man's Burden
(17, 2011)
Re-packaged AFRICOM Still not Good for Motherland
(21, 2010)
AFRICOM: US Military Control of Africa's Resources
(22, 2007)
AFRICOM and the Re-colonization of Africa (24, 2012)
AFRICOM Backs Bloodshed in Central Africa (25, 2010)
Resist AFRICOM – Puppet Masters (31, 2012)
The Imperial Agenda of the USA-AFRICOM Marches
On (31, 2012)
AFRICOM: Rise, Resist and Revolt (34, 2012)
Say No To AFRICOM Conspiracy (42, NA)
Rumble in the Jungle: The AFRICOM Boondoggle
(46, 2007)
Africom or Africon? (47, 2009)
AFRICOM: Devil in the Backyard (o/a 40, 2011)
AFRICOM off African Soil Petition (o/a 48, 2011)

Note: Search conducted on September 27, 2012.

**Box 4. Selected Headlines on AFRICOM
in First 50 Pages under Google Search
with Key Word "AFRICOM"
(Page of Appearance: Year of Article).**

In the future, military operations by U.S. forces on the African continent could damage African perceptions of AFRICOM most, particularly if this were to involve U.S. "boots on the ground." Combat operations were, of course, never excluded from AFRICOM's mandate, merely downplayed.[143] Operation ODYSSEY DAWN, while largely an air/naval operation that did not involve U.S. soldiers landing in Libya, was seized on by critics of AFRICOM as "proof" that the Command was, as they had always asserted, a wolf in sheep's clothing. Other Africans, however, did not oppose the Operation, because they were relieved to see the end of the 42-year Libyan dictatorship.

Part of the reason that AFRICOM's military operations have not generated strong, consistent resistance among sub-Saharan African stakeholders is that they have been in support of goals with which many Bantu Africans could identify. These include opposing the terrorist group Al-Qaeda in the Islamic Maghreb (AQIM) and Touareg allies who, in March 2012, took control of northern Mali from mainly the southern Mali-based, Bantu-speaking tribes that have dominated Mali's central government since independence. Similarly, the AFRICOM effort to aid the capture of Lord's Resistance Army leader Joseph Kony and its effort to support the AU's bid to rid Somalia of al-Shabaab are causes with which most Africans can identify.

One kind of AFRICOM "military operation" that could cause a strong African backlash in the future are intelligence, surveillance, and reconnaissance flights or kinetic operations by drones. The gist of a recent article in *The Washington Post* on U.S. drones reportedly being flown out of Djibouti[144] was widely re-reported in the African media. While AFRICOM's reported intelligence activities in the Sahel, and Central and East

Africa have avoided much criticism so far, they could eventually trigger strong African opposition, much as the increasingly obvious "drone wars" in Pakistan have triggered so much public condemnation in the Middle East. Consistent with this, a recent Africa Center for Strategic Studies report on Islamic militancy concluded in November 2012 that:

> Islamic militant organizations in African generally only command the support of small minorities within Muslim communities. However, ill-considered interventions, especially those involving Western forces, can reinforce the militant's narrative, thereby strengthening their credibility and recruitment.[145]

This analysis implies that AFRICOM must be cognizant of the possible, longer-term, unintended consequences of any military operations that it may undertake in Africa.

Already, multiple non-African sources consulted by the author were concerned that AFRICOM had already gone too far in emphasizing military operations versus its traditional focus on steady-state security engagement. To paraphrase one European colonel, "AFRICOM was once a good idea but has been hijacked by an increased focus on military operations." One senior U.S. Government source who preferred to remain anonymous decried an alleged focus at the Command on kinetic operations.

The author believes that AFRICOM's operations related to Libya, Somalia, the Lord's Resistance Army, and its current role in advising officials from the Economic Community of West African States involved in planning a multinational campaign to oust al-Qaeda in the Islamic Maghreb from northern Mali, indeed, have raised the profile of the Command's military operations, and could raise it further should the Special Operations Command in particular play a public role. It would be a mistake, however, to assert that AFRICOM had abandoned the "Plus" in CCMD Plus, as there has been no fundamental shift in the Command's orientation since the arrival of its current Commander, General Ham. In his November 21, 2012, presentation at Chatham House in London, General Ham stated:

> The priority tasks for—as outlined in the 2012 Defense Strategic Guidance—tell us that countering al-Qaida and violent extremists remain our highest priority, and that's understandable, I think, for a military organization. So those places in Africa where violent extremism exists or seems to be emerging are the areas of highest priority. I mentioned Somalia and the presence of al-Shabaab, Mali and the presence of Al-Qaida in the Islamic Maghreb, a growing network of variously named organizations across North and West Africa, and I would include in that Boko Haram and their presence in Nigeria as an area of increasing focus.

> . . . These are pressing and current issues, but we also recognize that these are not challenges that can be addressed exclusively through military means. While there may be a military component of a strategy to address violent extremism, military action in and of itself will not be successful. So what we really try to do more broadly across the continent with a regional focus is ensure that our military efforts are fully coordinated with a broader comprehensive strategy that addresses the underlying issues of instability. And those tend to focus on economic development, good governance, education.

Perhaps there is an inevitable pendulum swing in the life of any combatant command between steady-state engagement and military operations and that, in 2011-2012, there was a pronounced swing at AFRI-

COM toward military operations. As the above quote from General Ham indicates, however, the Command recognizes that African security challenges cannot be met long term by military means alone, but rather through a fully coordinated, comprehensive U.S. Government interagency strategy for Africa that addresses underlying, nonmilitary causes of instability.

If there has, in fact, been a swing toward military operations at AFRICOM, General Ham's quote also implies that this swing has not been due to the Commander's long-term intent, but rather reflects the contemporary, worsening security situation in some African countries. This security situation will hopefully improve over time—and arguably it already has in Somalia—thereby allowing a pendulum swing back at AFRICOM toward its traditional, longer-term capacity building through steady-state engagement.[146]

Is AFRICOM about U.S. Access to Africa's Energy Resources?

The author argued above that one geostrategic reason AFRICOM was created was Africa's growing economic importance in the world, both as a source of strategic natural resources, including oil, gas, and minerals, and as a market. Some critics of the Command—particularly in Africa—have repeatedly zeroed in on the energy aspect of U.S. interests in Africa and asserted that AFRICOM's central raison d'être was to help the United States "seize" natural resources in Africa. Academics framed this school of thought in terms of West African oil, but it applies equally to natural resource extraction throughout the continent:

Oil-related interventions since the end of the Cold War have been conceptualized in certain strands of academic debate as instances of a "new oil imperialism," within which struggles over oil have the potential to form a crucial axis of future Great Power conflict, especially between the U.S. and China.[147]

Why would some Africans and academics have such perceptions? There is no doubt that Africa is currently an important source of U.S. oil imports. By 2007, when AFRICOM was created, Angola and Nigeria had already become important suppliers of oil to the United States, and projections pointed toward the Gulf of Guinea region as a growing major source of U.S. energy imports.[148] One academic wrote in 2009 that considerable African oil:

> will be destined for the U.S., with tankers loading from offshore platforms and sailing directly across the Atlantic to terminals on the U.S eastern seaboard. Strategically, this is of major importance to the Americans since those shipments of crude are not exposed to disruption in the way that supplies from the volatile Middle East are. So improving maritime security in the Gulf of Guinea, and other areas is of supreme importance to the [United States].[149]

More recently, Dr. Peter Pham, a well-known Africa specialist at the Atlantic Council, wrote in July 2012 that:

> The current [Obama] administration's goal is to "eliminate our current imports from the Middle East and Venezuela within ten years." . . . The gap . . . will likely be made up by additional imports from Africa, where proved petroleum reserves have increased by 40 percent in the decade in contrast to the downward trends observed almost everywhere else.[150]

At present, the Gulf of Guinea is not only a major shipping route for global trade, but already the source of 18 percent of U.S. oil imports and 14 percent of its liquefied natural gas (LNG) imports. U.S. oil imports from Africa were 20 percent of total imports in 2011[151] and are expected to rise to 25 percent of total U.S. imports by 2015.[152]

Moreover, the economic importance of the U.S.-Africa relationship will increase as more countries in the sub-region discover oil and gas. In West Africa, new offshore oil and gas fields have been discovered recently in Ghana, Cote D'Ivoire, Liberia, Sierra Leone, and Sao Tome and Principe. Oil from the inland country of Chad is transported to international markets via a pipeline that ends in Cameroon, on the Gulf of Guinea, and there are prospects that oil discovered in the inland nations of Niger and (potentially) the Central African Republic would also be exported to global markets in the same way. In East Africa, there have also been recent oil and gas discoveries in Kenya, Uganda, Tanzania, and Mozambique that also point to the continent's increasing importance for global energy security.[153] Of course, most of this new oil will be exported to third markets, not the United States, but U.S. firms could also become involved as investors or partners in aspects of African oil and gas exploration, drilling, and pipeline construction and operation via various contractual, ownership, and production-sharing arrangements.

At the same time, it is important not to exaggerate the direct importance of Africa as a source of oil and gas for Washington. The use of new technologies such as hydraulic fracking and horizontal drilling have contributed to a new shale oil and gas boom in the United States, reducing its dependence on imports. According to the International Energy Agency's annual World Energy Outlook, U.S. oil production will peak at 11.1 million barrels per day in 2020, compared to 8.1 million barrels a day in 2011; U.S. oil imports are forecasted to decline to 4 million barrels per day from the current 10 million barrels per day. Since much of U.S. imports will be from North American suppliers Canada and Mexico, there will be a sharp drop in U.S. imports from Africa, reducing the strategic importance of Africa as an energy supplier to the United States.

Most importantly, however, just because U.S. oil imports from Africa are increasing for now does not mean that the United States is "seizing" this oil or that AFRICOM is a tool to accomplish this. Where some African (and non-African) observers err is in conflating interest by U.S. private-sector firms in the energy sector on the one hand, with U.S. Government security cooperation in Africa on the other. AFRICOM's mission statement and Commander's Intent in Box 3 are focused on human security, and nowhere mention energy security.

If anything, AFRICOM is actually *helping* Africa maximize the benefit of its natural resources by: 1) programs to help African littoral states build capacity to better control their own territorial waters and exclusive economic zones; and, 2) occasional innocent passage by U.S. naval vessels whose presence reinforces U.S. policy in favor of unimpeded access by boats and ships from all nations to international waters around Africa. AFRICOM, mainly through its Naval Forces Africa component, has been enabling long-term capacity building of African navies through its Africa Partnership Station program and joint exercises such as Saharan Express (north and west Africa), Obangame Express (west and central Africa), as well as joint training operations under the African Maritime Law Enforcement Program (for example, to stop illegal fishing and drug trafficking in West Africa). The DoD and AFRICOM have also taken such steps as selling an old Coast Guard cutter to Nigeria via DoD's Excess Defense Articles Program, helping Benin develop a national maritime strategy, and conducting a table-top exercise with Ghana to assist that nation in securing its new offshore oil platforms. The ships of the U.S. Navy's Sixth Fleet based in Naples, Italy, regularly patrol in the Mediterranean above North African territorial waters. The United States has also contributed to international anti-piracy efforts in the Horn of Africa along with several other nations.

For their part, U.S. energy producer and services companies are independent actors beholden to their global shareholders, not to AFRICOM or the U.S. Government. Far from "seizing" natural resources in Africa, these companies bring risk-capital, leading-edge technology and decades of experience into voluntary, arms-length transactions with African partners, in fierce competition with international rivals. Even when U.S. oil companies are active in Africa, either as equity investors or as part of long-term production-sharing agreements, they are generally outstanding corporate citizens—not part of the stereotyped, all-powerful "Seven Sisters" of the 1960s.[154] U.S. oil companies, like all U.S. firms, are constrained by strict anti-racketeering and anti-bribery laws in America, obliged to follow Organization for Economic Cooperation and Development (OECD) anti-corruption guidelines, and are watched closely by shareholder activists and U.S. civil society for their international compliance with strict environmental and labor norms. Overall, the oil firms are the best corporate citizens that African leaders and their publics could hope for.

Finally, most of the oil imported by the United States from Africa likely does not even involve U.S. equity oil, but rather is purchased on the global oil market from Africa parastatals, such as Sonangol in Angola, or from an increasingly large constellation of oil companies from Europe and developing countries, including China, Brazil, and Malaysia, that operate in Africa. Overall, this healthy global competition for African oil makes for more favorable terms of trade and improved investment terms for African nations (unless their citizens are sold out by bribe-taking elites).

In short, the fact that the United States is a good customer for African oil does not mean that Africa is losing, but rather gaining. The United States is neither "exploiting" Africa's natural resources, nor has AFRICOM acted as an "instrument" to allow this. One academic dismissed the "new oil imperialism" thesis previously introduced by stating, correctly, the author believes, that it:

> overemphasizes potential strategic conflicts without taking into account the ways in which the forms of globalization promoted by Washington since 1945 have actually served to reduce interstate conflict. Specifically, the US has long sought to 'transnationalize' economies in strategically important regions of the globe, rather than pursue a more mercantilist form of economic nationalism . . . thus embedding them into the broader global economy, which in turn opens them up to a broad array of investors on a non-discriminatory basis. . . . This global corporate presence in the region is fully aligned with U.S. interests: as long as the oil they produce is released onto world markets, investment and production by Malaysian, British, and Chinese companies contribute as much to U.S. energy security as do the activities of US companies themselves.[155]

Is AFRICOM Trying to Block China's Rise in Africa?

The above quote also responds convincingly to another recurring critique of AFRICOM—including one made interestingly by some Africans—that the Command somehow wishes to "block" China's rise in Africa and prevent Beijing from helping itself and its friends on the continent. One of the first questions asked of then Deputy Assistant Secretary of Defense (DASD) for Africa Policy Theresa Whelan, during a briefing on the new Africa Command in 2007, was *"Why was China missing from her briefing?"* DASD Whelan responded:

> It was missing for a reason, because this isn't about China. Everybody seems to want it to be about China and maybe that is a little nostalgia for the Cold War, I don't know. But it isn't about China. It is about U.S. security interests in Africa in the context of global security. China, yes, has become more engaged in Africa, both—primarily for economic reasons.[156]

It is ironic that AFRICOM, far from being a U.S. "tool" to keep China out of Africa, has actually facilitated China's prosperous entry into African markets, albeit in an indirect way. First, the assistance that AFRICOM brings to African militaries, including support for defense sector reform that aids the overall U.S. Government effort to support security sector reform, is helping countries on the continent to become more stable, thereby fostering an environment conducive to development and the very commercial opportunities that Chinese companies and individuals are exploiting successfully. Second, and as described above, AFRICOM is facilitating free access to the global commons, represented in this context primarily by the international waters around Africa, which benefits greatly Chinese shippers. In short, AFRICOM indirectly aids African development, much as the "Pax Americana" fostered by the U.S. military engagement in the Pacific has fostered stability and prosperity in East Asia since the end of World War II.

Moreover, if AFRICOM was created to "block" China from entering Africa, it has been a miserable failure. China-Africa trade passed the $1 billion mark in 1990, jumped to $10 billion in 2000, and accelerated again, increasing 15-fold in a little over a decade to $150 billion in 2011. China's rapidly expanding ties with Africa catapulted China past the United States in 2010 as Africa's top trading partner.[157] Ironically, it is also China—much more than the United States—that needs Africa as a source of oil to fuel its rapid industrialization and diversify supplies away from the volatile Middle East. One-third of its imports now come from the continent, versus only 18-19 percent for the United States.

At the end of the day, these critics of AFRICOM should be more concerned about what China brings to Africa, not what the United States brings. Aside from China's arms sales to nations such as Sudan, Western donors are concerned that the Chinese government's "no strings attached" approach to development risks undoing decades of Western efforts to promote good governance, revenue transparency, and responsible natural resource development in Africa; corrupts African elites; unfairly promotes China's interests at the expense of other non-African nations by violating OECD norms for aid and trade credits; free-rides on Highly Indebted Poor Country debt relief; and risks new unsustainable debts for African nations.[158]

While China's engagement with Africa has up to now been primarily led by the Chinese government and state-owned enterprises, nonstate actors, including privatized Chinese corporations and citizens, are also increasingly important. These nonstate actors are making a contribution to the diversity and depth of Chinese trade and investment with Africa, but are also aggravating a host of problems, including rampant corruption, the flouting of labor and environmental laws, and the sale of counterfeit goods. Large-scale immigration by Chinese to Africa — by some estimates totaling over one million persons — is creating tensions, particularly with African retail traders. Some African politicians and the continent's civil society are starting to debate the costs and benefits of China's growing economic ties with the continent.[159]

Does France Support or Oppose AFRICOM?

Some French officials and academics were also opposed to the creation of AFRICOM, which they saw as risking the export of the war on terror to Africa. Other observers have asserted that, for decades, France viewed its former colonies in Africa as an exclusive sphere of influence (pré carré). According to one U.S. academic, France actively lobbied its Western and Central African allies not to host AFRICOM headquarters and coordinated its efforts with the European Union (EU).[160] When Djibouti, a historical French ally, allowed the United States to establish a permanent base, some French viewed this decision the "new Fashoda,"[161] a historical reference to a UK military defeat of France in Africa. For some French, AFRICOM's creation as a sign that the era of exclusively French military influence in many of its former colonies was effectively over.[162]

Despite initial and perhaps visceral anti-American reactions in France against AFRICOM's creation, there were already two important ongoing trends in Paris that ultimately created a more favorable environment for this U.S. Command:

1. Successive recent French administrations, including those of Nicholas Sarkozy (President from May 2007 to May 2012) and the new French government of Francois Hollande, have stated publicly that France had abandoned its past *françafrique* policies under which Paris propped up dubious African regimes. Sarkozy, while campaigning for re-election in 2012, said that *françafrique* had become burdensome and that he wanted France to become more engaged in emerging markets in Asia and Latin America, which had greater potential for France's economic future.

2. Budgetary concerns and a changing strategic climate have also pushed France toward a multilateral approach. Structural changes in the armed forces—abandonment of the draft, sharp reductions in the size of the French military, and base closures between 1997 and 2002—have meant that France could no longer maintain the dominance it exercised in the 1960s and 1970s.

France's new military strategy in Africa, Andrew Hanson wrote:

> is one of 'prevention and projection,' which emphasizes using the smallest force possible, optimizing use of military technology, prioritizing intelligence, and pre-positioning forces in a region to respond quickly to crises—all of which are reflected in current African deployments.

Rachel Utley, a lecturer at the University of Leeds, has written that:

'France is still keen to exercise a leading role [in Africa],' says while offsetting the political, military, diplomatic, and financial costs of formerly **national** operations." France's remaining military presence in Africa, in terms of both bases and peace-keeping operations, are 'in the process of being **Europeanized**,' according to Brigadier General Dominique Trinquand, as France invites other European countries to commit forces to the bases (bolding added).

In conclusion, while there may have been military officials at France's *Ecole Militaire* headquarters in Paris who initially opposed AFRICOM's creation in 2007, they are fewer now. The reality for France is that budget cutbacks have forced it to reduce the size of its forces in Africa in recent years—including the base closure in Senegal announced in 2010. As the United States has increased its presence, both in terms of temporary engagements with African militaries and in terms of the opening and large expansion of its base in Djibouti, French military planners increasingly have recognized that AFRICOM's presence can actually be a huge boon for French interests.

In this regard, the March 2012 takeover of northern Mali by AQIM and its Touareg allies may also mark a watershed in a 180-degree turn in French attitudes about the Command. France sees Mali not only as a former colony, but as a nation so close to its own *metropole* that an al-Qaeda affiliate's takeover of the northern half of Mali represents a clear and present danger to the French homeland and Europe. In the UN, France played a central role in a resolution that gave 45 days to the Economic Community of West African States to come up with a credible intervention plan for northern Mali. In December 2012, press reports had indicated that France has been consulting with AFRICOM about what military planners and intelligence it could provide to support this plan—and how the United States could pay for it. As the Mali example suggests, France was moving not only to burden-share by "Europeanizing" its security policy in Africa, but to "Americanize" it as well, by welcoming AFRICOM's increased role on the continent and cutting back its own. France's sudden decision to intervene militarily in Mali on January 11, 2013, only corroborates the above conclusion, as it has since then pressed reluctant U.S. and European allies to provide Mali with air transport, air refueling, and intelligence support, while urging African troop contributions from its ally, Chad, and countries in West Africa.

PART V — THE FUTURE OF AFRICOM

In this concluding section, the author raises five issues important to AFRICOM's future: allocated forces, the selection of the Command's partner-nations, the desirability of regional approaches in Africa, the location of the Command's headquarters, and the need for a strategic right-sizing of the Command.

AFRICOM's Allocated Forces Do Not Equal Militarization of U.S. Foreign Policy.

With budgetary constraints looming and global priorities shifting, DoD recently published the *2012 Defense Strategic Guidance*, under which each geographic combatant command would be allocated or "aligned" an Army brigade to advise, train, and mentor partner-nation security forces throughout their respective areas of responsibility.[163] Not having aligned forces has been problematic for the Command. In attempting to plan its security cooperation efforts, AFRICOM found itself caught in an endless bureaucratic cycle of submitting requests for forces multiple times per year, often with no certainty that they would be provided.[164]

Because of this DoD initiative, AFRICOM will, for the first time starting in March 2013, have allocated forces that will deploy from bases in the continental United States to Africa on a rotational basis. For AFRICOM, a dedicated Regionally Aligned Brigade would expand on ongoing small-unit missions in Africa that are already being conducted either under the operational control of Special Operations Command-Africa or Marine Forces Africa. These include the Special Purpose Marine Air Ground Task Force of 200 Marines who are tasked to conduct theater security cooperation engagements and provide a limited crisis response capability from Sigonella, Italy.

For several years, AFRICOM's lack of allocated forces and the fact that it had to compete with requests for forces from other combatant commands hindered its efforts to foster strong military-to-military relationships in Africa and expand partner capacity building activities.[165] In the future, the 2nd Brigade Combat Team, 1st Infantry Division (2/1ID) out of Fort Riley, Kansas, will be AFRICOM's main go-to force provider for security cooperation missions in Africa. Soldiers within the 2/1ID, who were freed up following the Iraq and Afghanistan drawdowns in the Central Command, will remain at home in Kansas for most of the year they are aligned with AFRICOM. Teams that go to Africa as part of the alignment would typically be small, with mission lengths measured in weeks or months. During its first 6 months, 2/1ID is slated to participate in 96 activities in 34 countries—nearly two-thirds of the countries on the continent—and will receive language training in French, Arabic, and Swahili.[166]

What Americans might expect to be good news for Africa—the assignment of a Regionally Aligned Brigade to AFRICOM—could, instead, restoke fears among some Africans of the militarization of U.S. foreign policy and a prelude to U.S. military interventions on the continent. AFRICOM will have to socialize this concept with African partners in the coming months, explaining that the Brigade members will be present as small teams working across the continent and will not look much different than the way the Command currently provides security assistance.

Alliances with Autocratic African Leaders May be a Costly Error Later.

During the Cold War, the United States allied itself with several repressive, right wing governments as part of its global struggle with the Soviet Union. In Latin America, for example, it supported Chilean dictator Augusto Pinochet and the Argentinean military regimes. Not only were such unholy alliances inconsistent with the democratic values that Americans hold so dearly; they also exacerbated an anti-Americanism in Latin America that persists today. Similarly, perceived U.S. support for the apartheid regime in South Africa, as well as opposition to liberation movements in Angola, Namibia, and Zimbabwe in the 1960s to 1980s, left a legacy of strong anti-Americanism in several nations of southern Africa. This legacy, even today, has impeded and complicated U.S. efforts to foster stronger and deeper security ties to major African nations such as South Africa and Angola.

Analogous to what happened during the Cold War, the United States is partnering with repressive regimes in Africa in the name of anti-terrorism and stopping genocide, such as its backing of Uganda's support for the AU Mission in Somalia, Ethiopia's contributions to the UN Interim Security Force for Abyei, and support of Rwanda's troop contributions to the UN-African Union Mission in Darfur. In the early-1990s, the United States identified several so-called Renaissance leaders of Africa. They included figures such as Yoweri Museveni of Uganda, Meles Zenawi of Ethiopia, and Paul Kagame of Rwanda, whom the United States hoped would usher in a new era of sound, democratic governance.[167] What started out well is going badly, as the United States has continued to support all three of these new leaders even as they become increasingly autocratic. While the United States did recently (and likely temporarily) distance itself from President Kagame following a recent UN report describing the collusion between the Rwandan government and M-23 rebels who are destabilizing the eastern Democratic Republic of the Congo, Washington has continued to embrace Uganda's Museveni for his troop contributions to the AU Mission in Somalia, and for his cooperation in hunting Lord's Resistance Army leader Kony. As part of its efforts to support the AU's fight against al-Shabaab, the United States also worked closely with Ethiopian long-time autocratic leader Meles Zenawi who, during his 21-year rule, denied that country any chance to start to develop a real democratic tradition.[168]

Defenders of current U.S. policy might respond with considerable validity that, up to now, the United States has had to rely heavily on autocratic regimes in Ethiopia, Uganda, and Rwanda because they contribute the bulk of, and some of the most capable, troops to the AU Mission to Somalia and to the UN-AU Mission in Darfur.[169] Moreover, they might add that both Missions were early 2007 "coalitions of the willing" that predated the establishment of AFRICOM (while the UN Interim Security Force in Abyei is a newer creation).[170]

What can the United States do differently? Are there really any alternatives to partnering with autocratic Africa leaders on peacekeeping? The answer, in the short term, is no. For now, staying involved and providing training to include International Military Education and Training may help influence future leaders to follow the rule of law better. However, over the longer term, there is no *force majeur* reason—no Cold War imperative—why the United States and its Africa Command should feel compelled to work so closely with African "big men." While it will require patience and determination, the U.S. Government should try in the future—to the extent there are potential troop-contributing countries for a given mission—to give clearer priority to emerging democracies in Africa, such as the Benins of the continent, in choosing future partner-nations for the training of African peacekeepers. As noted above, with the collapse of the Soviet Union in early-1991, African countries were freed from Cold War clientelism. These events set off a multi-year wave of political liberalization that started in 1990 with Benin's national conference and led to an increasing number of emerging democracies on the continent. The United States needs to choose from this increasing universe of emerging African democracies for its peacekeeping training — a policy shift that would also reinforce the principle of civilian-led militaries in these new, democratic societies.

As a nation, we do Leahy vetting to ensure that *individuals* who receive U.S. military training are not past human rights violators.[171] As a nation, we should also try to be more selective in vetting nations that we choose to train for AU and UN peacekeeping missions. At the same time, however, the practical challenges of finding suitable troop-contributing countries may make this goal idealistic and elusive. African countries that are both emerging democracies and willing and capable to contribute troops, even with additional training, are relatively few. The U.S. political system already prevents the U.S. Government from providing peacekeeping training for the most egregious African regimes, such as Eritrea or Zimbabwe. While training peacekeepers for the AU Mission in Somalia from an increasingly autocratic regime like that of Uganda is not ideal, these peacekeepers have allowed the United States to advance other important peace and security, and counterterrorism goals on the rest of the continent. It is easy to imagine that without the participation (and sacrifices) of the Uganda People's Defence Force in Somalia, al-Shabaab would still be in charge in Mogadishu today and represent a threat to the U.S. homeland.

AFRICOM Strengthening Regional Approaches.

One way to alleviate African concerns about AFRICOM would be to further strengthen the Command's commitment to support regional approaches to Africa's security problems. Recognizing this, AFRICOM has already expanded many of its programs and exercises to help the AU and five of its Regional Economic Communities develop the AU's African Peace and Security Architecture.[172] AFRICOM should continue to increase training assistance on multilateral terms through the African Standby Force and its five regional brigades, e.g., through battalion and brigade-level exercises, command post exercises, and U.S.-supported peace training centers in each region.[173] Consistent with this, AFRICOM's Commander told Congress in February 2012 that the Command will:

> Seek new ways to work with and through the African Union and its regional organizations and to support their leadership in preventing and responding to African security challenges.[174]

AFRICOM should also ensure stronger coordination with the UN Department of Peacekeeping Operations in New York, working with and through the DoS and the U.S. Mission to the UN, in order to avoid duplication of effort with other donors and to provide a coherent international plan for training and mobilizing African peacekeepers.

Where Should AFRICOM be Headquartered?

In events with African audiences and the African press, the issue of the location of AFRICOM's headquarters remains a perennial favorite. Since its inception, the question of AFRICOM's headquarters has been like a powerful two-sided magnet. On the one side, AFRICOM was repulsive to many Africans, who rejected having the Command on African soil for the reasons noted previously. On the other side, members of the U.S. Congress covet the prestige, dollars, and jobs that military basing brings. Several members, including those from South Carolina, Virginia, Georgia, and Texas, have expressed the desire to have AFRICOM move to their districts.

Both to deflect African questions and Congressional pressure, then Secretary of Defense Robert Gates indicated in 2007 that the "final" decision on AFRICOM's location would be deferred for 5 years, until 2012. While the DoD has still not made this decision, the then AFRICOM Commander, General Ham, did confirm in September 2012 that the United States would not, for the foreseeable future, establish the headquarters of AFRICOM in any part of the African continent, ostensibly due to the heavy financial cost of doing so:

> There have been some African countries that have quietly made it known that should the United States be willing to establish AFRICOM base in Africa they might be willing to hand us a place. There are also other African countries who have made it known clearly that they do not want AFRICOM to be based in their country or the African continent. Today, the reality is that we have found ourselves in a financial situation that it will be too costly to situate our new headquarters anywhere on the continent of Africa.[175]

To some extent, the Commander's financial explanation why AFRICOM would not be based in Africa is partly disingenuous diplomacy. True, there would be real and extremely high economic costs of establishing and operating a combatant command staff headquarters in Africa. These include the enormous costs of purchasing or leasing long-term offices, housing, and security-related infrastructure to assure Western standards of living and force protection, and the extremely high transportation costs of intra-African air travel (which must often be accomplished by flying first to Europe, and then back to the continent). However, the reality is that for political reasons—and regardless of cost—the United States could not place its staff headquarters for AFRICOM in Africa. To attempt to do so would have created endless opposition from certain African countries, including regional hegemons who would perceive a permanent American military presence as an unwelcome incursion into their spheres of influence. Not surprisingly, only smaller African countries such as Liberia have shown any *public* enthusiasm for hosting AFRICOM, both for the economic benefits it would bring, and because they believe that the United States could serve as a counterweight to their own regional hegemon.

Will AFRICOM stay where it is, or move back to the United States? For now, it is destined to remain in the northern European city of Stuttgart, Germany, which, *The Economist* amusingly pointed out, is several thousands of miles from Africa's northern boundary along the Mediterranean Sea [and] "a sleepy and dour town in Germany that is perhaps the least African place in the world."[176]

Why stay put? Stuttgart, where the U.S. European Command still resides, is a logical place to keep AFRICOM. While the costs of operating a combatant command in Europe are enormous, the existing infrastructure for the Command is already there, and millions of dollars (in admittedly sunk costs) have already been spent to refurbish and improve Kelley Barracks, where AFRICOM is located. Stuttgart also has the advantage of being in the same time zone as much of Africa, whereas a based located in the United

States would have to address time zone differences from Washington that, at various times of year due to daylight savings time, range from 4 to 9 hours. Air connections to Africa, via short stops in various European capitals, are excellent.

Consistent with this, Army General Martin Dempsey, Chairman of the Joint Chiefs of Staff, told an AFRICOM audience in December 2012 that he thought the Command should stay in Stuttgart and that:

> We think for operational reasons—unless there is a huge (cost) disparity—operational reasons should dominate [the debate about location].[177]

This being said, it may be worthwhile to shift AFRICOM's headquarters back to the United States in the years to come. The tipping point may arrive as intra-African air service improves in frequency and safety, and as air connections between the U.S. East Coast and various African capitals improve.

Why the Threat of U.S. Strategic Insolvency Means AFRICOM Must Right-Size; and Why Intelligence Expenditures and Intelligence, Surveillance, and Reconnaissance Assets Merit Cost-Benefit Scrutiny.

An academic at the U.S. National War College, Michael Mazarr, argued in the fall of 2012 that:

> Throughout history, major powers have confronted painful inflection points when their resources, their national will, or the global geopolitical context no longer sustained their strategic postures" [and that] 'the post-war U.S. approach to strategy is rapidly becom-

ing insolvent and unsustainable [and that insolvency]
will finally come true over the next five to ten years,
unless we adjust much more fundamentally.[178]

Mazarr sees the United States as an overextended
superpower, and likened the current U.S. position to
that of Great Britain in the 1890s—the world's global
power at the time, but one that kept on making commitments overseas to the point that it simply could not
afford them any longer.[179] At a time when the United
States is chronically running more than trillion dollar
annual budget deficits and when geopolitical changes
include the rise of China as an unpredictable global
partner and rival, there is a real risk for the United
States of "strategic insolvency." In this context, every
part of the U.S. Government should be re-examined
and justified or cut back—including the $688.2 billion
in Pentagon budgetary outlays in Fiscal Year 2012.[180]

A June 2011 DoD report on the organizational
structure of combatant commands claimed that AF-
RICOM's headquarters staffing was not sufficient
for full-time operational capacity during an extend-
ed crisis—and, by implication, that AFRICOM staff
should be increased. The report stated, for example,
that during Operation ODYSSEY DAWN in Libya,
AFRICOM's headquarters was augmented by 90 personnel, and that additional personnel would have been
required to maintain continuous operations if Operation ODYSSEY DAWN had continued longer than it
did. [181] Mazarr might argue that the DoD's June 2011
report was an example of the old way of doing busi-
ness: more staff and a bigger budget as the "solution"
to every "problem," instead of looking at "strategic
opportunity costs"(and recognizing that the budgetary and other) "factors closing down on the current

paradigm are not merely momentary or reversible—they are structural."[182]

It is argued that AFRICOM was finally created in 2007 because the continent's time of strategic importance to the United States had finally arrived. Ironically, the Command may also prove to be one of the many commitments that the United States made but could not really afford because its existing commitments—including a decade of wars in Afghanistan and Iraq—were already so costly. The solution is also not to close down AFRICOM, which costs a pittance compared to the overall DoD budget, but to seek cost savings to make the Command's operations more efficient. One way to do this would be to undertake a top-down right-sizing exercise, including a possible reduction in its overall staffing. AFRICOM 's J-2 directorate, with a large staff spread between Stuttgart, Molesworth, and Tampa, may be a Directorate that could be scaled back. The DoS Bureau of Intelligence and Research office following Africa has a staff of only about 15 professionals, while AFRICOM's J-2 staff numbers several hundred and does not include analysts at the DIA in Washington who also cover the continent.

AFRICOM's Commander testified before Congress in February 2012 that intelligence, surveillance, and reconnaissance (ISR) assets:

> are a key enabler for many of our operations and engagements [and that assets] based in Sigonella, Italy, and Souda Bay, Greece, were used in Operation ODYSSEY DAWN and NATO Operation UNIFIED PROTECTOR and continue to be used today to monitor illegal trafficking and violent extremist organizations.[183]

While acknowledging the value of these assets, AFRICOM could also look closely at related programs to see if they are cost-effective, including seeking lessons learned from surveillance and reconnaissance efforts earlier in the Command's history that may not have resulted in actionable intelligence. For example, *The Washington Post* reported in June 2012 on two contractor-based Missions: "Creek Sand" in Mali, which was reportedly aimed at AQIM and "Tusker Sand" in Central Africa, which reportedly aimed at locating Lord's Resistance Army leader Kony.[184] In this regard, a senior AFRICOM official told the author that the Command had made adjustments in 2012 to rationalize its ISR efforts.[185] It is likely that AFRICOM-funded intelligence has been used effectively to assist France after its January 11, 2013, decision to intervene militarily in northern Mali against AQIM, but only an honest internal assessment can determine if overall AFRICOM intelligence monies have been well spent.

ENDNOTES

1. The U.S. Pacific Command was founded in January 1947 and the U.S. European Command in March 1947. The other geographic combatant commands besides U.S. Africa Command (AFRICOM) were founded as follows: the U.S. Southern Command (1963), the U.S. Central Command (1983), and the U.S. Northern Command (2002). There have been other geographic combatant commands (CCMD) that no longer exist, such as the Atlantic Command and the Far East Command. See *en.wikipedia.org/wiki/Unified_Combatant_Command#History*.

2. Claudia Anyaso, "An Overview of AFRICOM: A Unified Combatant Command," DISAM Journal of International Security Assistance Management, September 2008.

3. Gilbert Taguem Fah, "Dealing with AFRICOM: The Political Economy of Anger and Protest," *The Journal of Pan African Studies*, Vol. 3, No. 6, March 2010.

4. Sean McFate, "US Africa Command: Next Step or Next Stumble," *African Affairs*, December 24, 2007, pp. 111-120.

5. During the Cold war, there were a limited number of U.S. troops stationed in Morocco (including Nouasseur Air Base near Casablanca, Rabat Salé Air Base, and Port Lyautey, north of Rabat, until the early-1960s), and Libya (Wheelus Air Base near Tripoli until 1970), where they focused on dissuading Soviet threats. From the end of World War II through the 1970s, there also was a large communications relay facility, Kagnew Station, in Asmara, Ethiopia, which today is in Eritrea.

6. In 1960, the Department of Defense (DoD) included Sub-Saharan Africa in the U.S. Atlantic Command, leaving North Africa in the European Command. Sub-Saharan Africa was later shifted in 1962 to a newly-created Strike Command, which was renamed as Readiness Command in 1971, at which point sub-Saharan Africa was again left outside the combatant command structure.

7. Under Central Command were Djibouti, Egypt, Eritrea, Ethiopia, Kenya, Somalia, and Sudan; under the Pacific Command were the Comoros, Madagascar, Mauritius, and the Seychelles. See also Lauren Ploch, "African Command: U.S. Strategic Interest and the Role of the U.S. Military in Africa," Washington, DC: Congressional Research Service, July 22, 2011, p. 14.

8. With the fall of the Berlin wall in 1989 and the collapse of the Soviet Union in early-1991, African countries were freed from Cold War clientelism. These events set off a multi-year wave of political liberalization that started in 1990 with Benin's national conference and led to an increasing number of emerging democracies on the continent. These political changes, while positive, did not change DoD views of Africa's lack of strategic importance.

9. As quoted from Ploch, "African Command," p. 14.

10. The African Center for Strategic Studies is located in Washington, DC, and is one of five DoD regional centers.

11. Milady Ortiz, "U.S. Africa Command: A New Way of Thinking," *National Security Watch*, March 13, 2008, p. 3.

12. *Ibid.*, p. 2. There was actually an earlier call for an Africa Command made in 1997 by Dr. C. William Fox, a military physician and then lieutenant colonel, who wrote "Military Medical Operations in Sub-Saharan Africa: The DoD 'Point of the Spear' for a New Century," available from *vincecrawley.wordpress.com/2011/08/31/journey-to-africom/*. Dr. Fox (Major General, Ret.) also published a version of this study by Carlisle, PA: Strategic Studies Institute, U.S. Army War College, 1997, available from *www.strategicstudiesinstitute.army.mil/pubs/display.cfm?pubID=202*.

13. McFate.

14. Advance questions for General Bantz J. Craddock, nominee for U.S. European Command and Supreme Allied Commander, Europe, in hearing before Senate Armed Services Committee, September 19, 2006.

15. At Secretary Donald Rumsfeld's direction, the formal study began in the summer of 2006, with a recommendation going to the White House concurrent with Rumsfeld's resignation in December 2006, the former AFRICOM Public Affairs Deputy told the author on November 19, 2012. One source who was a senior DoD official in the Office of the Secretary of Defense for several years, including the period 2006-07, told the author that the CCMDs and the Pentagon Joint Staff were actually strongly opposed to the creation of AFRICOM in order to protect their bureaucratic turf, and that:

> the only reason AFRICOM was created was because Rumsfeld wanted it . . . [the European Command] was particularly opposed because they saw it as taking resources from their command. [the Central Command] was less adamant about it because they were distracted by Iraq and Afghanistan.

The author imagines that Pacific Command opposition to AFRICOM's creation was even weaker than the Central Command's, given that its territorial loss was only the large island nation of Madagascar and three small island nations of the Comoros, Mauritius, and the Seychelles. Whatever the reality of turf battles at the time, however, the Bush announcement of its intention of creating a U.S. Command for Africa was ultimately delayed until early-2007, when the Ethiopian invasion of Somalia against the Islamic Courts played out.

16. Available from *www.africom.mil.*

17. A new terrorism group in Nigeria, Boko Haram, while important now, only existed in a nascent form in 2007, and is not discussed here. ("Boko" means "Western, secular education" in Hausa; and "Haram" means "sinful" in Arabic.)

> The group was established around 2002 by Mohammed Yusuf, a self-educated activist . . . . and Salafi scholar Jafar Mahmou Adam . . . . While Boko Haram repeatedly clashed with Nigerian security forces in a low-intensity conflict beginning in 2003, the violence intensified . . . . after Yusuf was killed by Nigerian police in 2009. [Boko Haram] gained worldwide attention with the suicide bombing of the United Nation's headquarters in Abuja in August 2011.

Terje Ostebo, "Islamic Militancy in Africa," ACSS Africa Security Brief No. 23, November 2012, p. 2.

18. Available from *en.wikipedia.org/wiki/Osama_bin_Laden.*

19. Perhaps the first international terrorist group in Africa in recent times, the Armed Islamic Movement was founded in 1982 in Algeria, after Islamists—who had been active in Algeria's first political party, founded in 1962 and derived from the anti-French liberation movement—began to simmer with resentment. This occurred after they were marginalized, starting in the late-1970s, by the government's increasingly secular policies and concentration of power by the military elite. The Movement splintered in 1987 after its leader was killed by security forces and in the wake of so-called "couscous rights," which led to multiparty elections and the founding of the Islamic Salvation Front in 1989. By the early-1990s, hundreds of Algerian militants who had trained and, in some cases, fought in Afghanistan against the Soviets began returning to Algeria, and sought an Islamist state. In 1992, some of these "Afghan Arabs," outraged by the Algerian military's deposal of Algeria's President, declaration of a state of emergency, and crackdown on Islamists in 1992, helped cause a schism in the Front and founded the Armed Islamic Group later that year. This group, in turn, split off in 1998 into the Islamist Group for Preaching and Combat, which was then rebranded in 2007 as Al-Qaeda in the Islamic Maghreb (AQIM) after declaring its allegiance to

bin Laden. For more detail, see Stephen Harmon, "From GSPC to AQIM: The Evolution of an Algerian Islamist Terrorist Group into an Al Qaida Affiliate," Concerned Africa Scholars, Bulletin No. 85, Spring 2010.

20. Ostebo, p. 2.

21. U.S. security interests in Somalia can be traced back to the Cold War. In 1969, a Somali general took power in a *coup d'état*, declared himself President and allied himself with the Soviet Union. He changed course in 1978, however, when his Government sought U.S. aid in its war with Ethiopia, which itself had fallen into the Soviet orbit after the overthrow in 1973 of Emperor Haile Selasse. By the late-1980s, various clan factions and sub-factions opposed his autocratic rule and forced him from power in early-1991. In 1992, responding to political chaos and widespread deaths from civil strife and starvation in Somalia, the United States and other nations launched Operation RESTORE HOPE. This was followed by the the United Nations (UN) operation in Somalia. See *www.state.gov/r/pa/ei/bgn/2863.htm*.

22. See *en.wikipedia.org/wiki/Al-Shabaab_(militant_group)*.

23. See *en.wikipedia.org/wiki/Al-Qaeda_involvement_in_Africa*.

24. While greatly weakened, al-Shabaab remains a potent force and may recreate itself as an insurgency, thereby hampering the new Somali Government's ability to finally assert its authority over most of the country's national territory. It had many foreigners within its ranks, particularly at the leadership level. As of 2010, their number was estimated to be between 200 and 300, augmented by around 1,000 diasporan ethnic Somalis. Among the foreign leaders was Fazul Abdullah Mohammed, a Kenyan national, who was appointed by Osama bin Laden as al-Qaeda's leader in East Africa in late 2009 and killed by Somali Transitional Federal Government forces in June 2011. Fazul was the last of the three al-Qaeda operatives wanted for the 1998 suicide attacks on the U.S. embassies in Kenya and Tanzania to have been killed. In September 2009, U.S. Special Operations Forces, acting in coordination with AFRICOM, killed Saleh Ali Saleh Nabhan during a raid south of Mogadishu. In early-2007, Abu Tahla al Sudani was killed during fighting with Ethiopian forces.

25. See also section on oil diplomacy in David E. Brown, *Hidden Dragon, Crouching Lion: How China's Advance in Africa is Underestimated and Africa's Potential Underappreciated*, Carlisle, PA: Strategic Studies Institute, U.S. Army War College, September 2012.

26. Charles W. Hooper, "Going Farther By Going Together—Building Partner Capacity in Africa," *Joint Forces Quarterly*, Issue 67, 4th quarter 2012, pp. 9, 12.

27. Ortiz, p. 3.

28. "Actions Needed to Address Stakeholder Concerns, Improve Interagency Collaboration, and Determine Full Costs Associated with the U.S. Africa Command," GAO-09-181, Washington, DC: U.S. Government Accounting Office (GAO) February 2009, p. 28.

29. McFate.

30. Donna Miles, "AFRICOM's Makeup Promotes 'Whole-of-Government' Approaches," *American Forces Press Service*, July 2, 2012, available from *www.defense.gov/news/newsarticle. aspx?id=116982*.

31. Lauren Ploch, "AFRICOM: Rationales, Roles, and Progress on the Eve of Operations," Washington, DC: Committee on Oversight and Government Reform: Subcommittee on National Security and Foreign Affairs, July 15, 2008.

32. Ploch, "African Command."

33. In December 2005, the White House issued National Security Presidential Directive 44, which recognized the primacy of reconstruction and stabilization operations, and forms the foundation for interagency coordination of all stability and reconstruction programs. One month earlier, the Pentagon had issued Department of Defense Directive 3000.05, "Military Support for Stabilization, Security, Transition, and Reconstruction Operations," which defined stability operations as a "core U.S. military mission" that "shall be given priority comparable to combat operations."

34. Carter Ham, "Posture Statement of U.S. Africa Command," Washington, DC: House Armed Services Committee, February 29, 2012.

35. J. Peter Pham, "Africa in the 'New, New World'," *Atlantic Council*, July 19, 2012.

36. "Improved Planning, Training, and Interagency Collaboration Could Strengthen DOD's Efforts in Africa," GAO-10-794, Washington, DC: GAO, July 2010, p. 5. The DoD defines *stability operations* as "military and civilian activities conducted across the spectrum from peace to conflict to establish or maintain order in States and regions." See also Ploch, "AFRICOM: Rationales, Roles, and Progress on the Eve of Operations."

37. See *en.wikipedia.org/wiki/Human_security*.

38. See *en.wikipedia.org/wiki/R2P*.

39. One congressional source felt that AFRICOM had paid lip service to R2P, but that its actual role to date has been limited to Libya and the counter-Lord's Resistance Army missions, despite ongoing atrocities in places like Sudan. The author believes, however, that decisions that a combatant command should intervene to prevent mass atrocities are ultimately political decisions, not military ones.

40. See *www.africom.mil/AboutAFRICOM.asp*.

41. Carter Ham, "Commander's Intent," Kelley Barracks, Stuttgart, Germany, August 2011.

42. *Ibid.*

43. GAO-10-794, July 2010, p. 6.

44. The term "jointness" here is an allusion to the Goldwater-Nichols Department of Defense Reorganization Act of 1986, which attempted to fix problems caused by interservice rivalry between the Army, Navy, Air Force, and Marines. Problems caused by interservice rivalry emerged during the Vietnam War, contributed

to the catastrophic failure of the Iranian hostage rescue mission in 1980, and were still evident in the invasion of Grenada in 1983. Some of the early misgivings within the U.S. Government about AFRICOM's creation may have stemmed from the fact that DoD was willing to carry out a major experiment in whole-of-government approaches, while other agencies were unwilling to have a U.S. military entity become the principal integrating agent, an early AFRICOM public affairs official told the author on November 19, 2012.

45. The other five geographic CCMDs are the U.S. European, Central, Pacific, Southern, and Northern Commands.

46. CCMDs are led by a four-star general or admiral, and are "joint" units, meaning they control forces from multiple services (Army, Navy, Air Force, and Marines). The unified combatant CCMDs originated during the Cold War, and were designed to better coordinate and integrate U.S. military forces for armed confrontation against the Soviet Union and its proxies. The U.S. military has two types of unified CCMDs: those responsible for territory (six total) and those responsible for a function (three total), of which there are the U.S. Special Operations Command, the U.S. Strategic Command, and the U.S. Transportation Command. A fourth functional CCMD, the U.S. Joint Forces Command, was disestablished in August 2011. The new U.S. Cyber Command gained initial operating capacity in May 2010, but is a sub-unified Command subordinate to the U.S. Strategic Command.

47. It is a common to speak of Africa's "54" nations, but this is a political, not geographic, characterization. The African Union (AU) does indeed have 54 member-states with the addition of the new nation of South Sudan in July 2011. However, Morocco is not an AU member because of the sensitive issue of the Western Sahara. Therefore, Africa actually has 55 nations—not 54. At the same time, AFRICOM has only 54 nations in its area of responsibility because Egypt is in the Central Command.

48. While Egypt is officially part of the Central Command, AFRICOM officials often informally consult with their Egyptian counterparts about security issues of significance to both Cairo and Washington in the rest of Africa.

49. Personnel staffing numbers, except for Combined Joint Task Force-Horn of Africa, are from "U.S. Africa Command, Command Brief," Lieutenant Colonel Robert W. Borja, USAF, AFRICOM Liaison Office, September 12 , 2012.

50. *The Washington Post* reported in October 2012 that there were about 3,200 U.S. troops, civilians, and contractors at Camp LeMonnier—apparently a significant increase in personnel since 2010. See Craig Whitlock, "Secret Ops Grow at U.S. Base," *The Washington Post*, October 26, 2012.

51. Camp Lemonnier is distinct from Combined Joint Task Force-Horn of Africa, which is an organization housed on the installation. The Combined Joint Task Force accounts for just over 50 percent of the U.S. personnel and assets at Camp Lemonnier, per a former Deputy Public Affairs Officer at AFRICOM.

52. Lauren Ploch, "African Command: U.S. Strategic Interest and the Role of the U.S. Military in Africa," Washington, DC: Congressional Research Service, July 22, 2011.

53. Formerly known as Operation ENDURING FREEDOM—TRANS-SAHEL.

54. *Ibid.*

55. Six weeks after September 11, 2001, then Secretary of Defense Rumsfield authorized the creation of CCMD-level Joint Interagency Coordination Groups. This Paper only compares AFRICOM to the Southern and Pacific Commands. It was actually the Central Command, however, that created the first CCMD-level Joint Interagency Coordination Groups on November 20, 2001, when it created a Joint Interagency Task Force-Counterterrorism. By February 2003, this Central Command joint group had 54 non-military members, including the Department of Energy, Treasury's Office of Foreign Asset Control, the Internal Revenue Service, and State's International Information Programs bureau. This was actually a larger interagency contingent than AFRICOM's, but proportionally smaller given the Central Command's much larger size. In July 2004, the Central Command's joint group began reporting directly to the Deputy Commander. The following month, the Central Command established an "Interagency Execu-

tive Steering Group" focusing on operational issues. Chaired by the Deputy Commander, co-chaired by the Command's Political Advisor, and staffed by the Command's directors and senior DoD and other agency representatives, this group was intended to guide the Command's interagency coordination efforts. While an innovation, Central Command's Joint Interagency Coordination Group appears to have been created more to inform the Commander than to boost Central Command coordination with the interagency. See Bogdanos, p. 3, 14.

56. Ploch, "African Command."

57. A number of articles on AFRICOM assert that DoD originally proposed that *one-half* of the AFRICOM's headquarters staff come from the interagency, but the author has found no original source documents corroborating this assertion. By contrast, a more authoritative source, a 2009 GAO study, indicated that the initial goal was to have *one-quarter* of staff from the DoD. See "Actions Needed to Address Stakeholder Concerns, Improve Interagency Collaboration, and Determine Full Costs Associated with the U.S. Africa Command," GAO-09-181, Washington, DC: GAO, February 2009, highlights.

58. Donna Miles, "AFRICOM's Makeup Promotes 'Whole-of-Government' Approaches," *American Forces Press Service*, July 2, 2012, available from *www.defense.gov/news/newsarticle. aspx?id=116982*.

59. Steven Olson and David Anderson, "Building Interagency Capabilities at U.S. Africa Command," *InterAgency Journal*, Vol. 2, No. 2, 2011.

60. Comments made to the author by anonymous interagency source in 2011.

61. Of course, any legislation promoting new jointness should apply to all national security/foreign policy agencies, not just non-DoD agencies.

62. As part of its initial attempt to market itself as a "different combatant command," AFRICOM eschewed the Pentagon's tra-

ditional J-Code structure, a method of organizing a Command for warfighting adopted by Napoleon. The J-Codes are:

1 - personnel and administration
2 - intelligence and security
3 - operations
4 - logistics
5 - plans
6 - communications or IT
7 - training,
8 - finance and contracts; also known as "resource management"
9 - Civil-Military Cooperation or "civil affairs"

For example, AFRICOM's J-5 was known only as "Strategy, Plans, and Programs." However, with the arrival of AFRICOM's second Commander, General Ham, in March 9, 2011, and the advent of the AFRICOM-led Operation ODYSSEY DAWN in Libya only 11 days later, the Command reverted to using J-Codes to describe its Directorates. This may have been in part to avoid confusion within other Commands, such as the European and Southern Commands, which had to support AFRICOM with temporary duty personnel. Southern Command reportedly had made an earlier shift away from J-Codes, only to revert back to them after the new directorate names proved confusing to outsiders during crisis management.

63. As described to the author by AFRICOM J-5 Deputy Director James Hart, Rear Admiral (Ret.), January 2, 2013.

64. In late-2010/early-2011, the DoS new Conflict and Stabilization Operations Bureau established two positions in the command—one each in the J3 (vacant) and J5 (filled). A natural synergy existed in embedding an officer from this new Bureau in the Command given AFRICOM's emphasis on conflict prevention, and this Bureau's own desire to expand U.S. Government expeditionary capability (including through the use of the interagency Civilian Response Corps).

65. Both heads of AFRICOM's J-9 have been senior Foreign Service Officers (FSO) at the Minister-Counselor (O-8 equivalent) rank, one of whom was an ambassador and both of whom were Public Affairs cone officers.

66. Within the DoS the Political-Military Bureau is the principal link to the DoD; it provides policy direction in the areas of international security, security assistance, military operations, defense strategy and plans, and defense trade. See State Department, October 5, 2012, intranet website description of Political-Military Bureau.

67. Joseph Cerano *et al.*, eds., *Rethinking Leader and "Whole of Government" National Security Reform: Problems, Progress, and Prospects*, Carlisle, PA: Strategic Studies Institute, U.S. Army War College, May 2010, p. 44.

68. The promotion precepts for the DoS Foreign Service Generalist and Specialist Corps define senior ranks as those at FS-1 (Generalist) or FP-1 (Specialist) or above, while "senior" in other contexts can refer to officers in the Senior Foreign Service (OC or above), i.e., equivalent to the military's General and Flag Officer ranks.

69. The Agency for International Development is part of the DoS. Its Agency head carries the equivalent rank to that of a Deputy Secretary of State and reports to the Secretary of State. The Agriculture Department has a Foreign Agricultural Service, and the Commerce Department has a Foreign Commercial Service whose members are also FSOs.

70. GAO 2010, p. 30; and *www.africom.mil*.

71. Miles, "AFRICOM's Makeup Promotes 'Whole-of-government' Approaches."

72. These codes start with the letter "J," since AFRICOM is a "joint" services Command with staff from the Army, Navy, Air Force, and Marines.

73. There were also discussions in AFRICOM about transforming Combined Joint Task Force-Horn of Africa into a Joint Interagency Task Force to provide interagency coordination of the Command's activities in the Horn of Africa, but this idea has yet to be implemented.

74. All three Foreign Policy Advisors who have served at AFRICOM have been Africa specialists at the rank of Counselor or Minister-Counselor (O-7 or O-8 equivalents).

75. John Pendleton, "Force Structure—Preliminary Observations on the Progress and Challenges Associated with Establishing the U.S. Africa Command," Testimony before the Subcommittee on National Security and Foreign Affairs, Committee on Oversight and Government Reform, U.S. House of Representatives, July 15, 2008, GAO-08-947T.

76. GAO-09-181, February 2009, p. 36.

77. Some military officers at AFRICOM were uncomfortable with the title of the Deputy to the Commander for Civil-Military Activities and sought clarification of the incumbent's authority. The Command has clarified that this Deputy has no Title 10 authority and no "command authority" over uniformed personnel, a former AFRICOM Public Affairs official told the author on November 19, 2012. Some have used this clarification of Title 10 authority to further question if the two Deputies can be considered "co-equals." However, there was never any intention for this Deputy to direct military operations, which as their respective titles imply, was the purview of the Deputy Commander for Military Operations. While true that the responsibilities of the two Deputies are different, they are considered in the AFRICOM hierarchy to both be Deputies to the Commander and have been repeatedly described in Congressional testimony and other public documents as co-equals. Analogously, there are now two Deputy Secretaries of State, one of whom oversees USAID. They are of equal rank and simply fill different functions.

78. Per the AFRICOM website, available from *www. africom.mil.*

79. AFRICOM's three Deputy Commanders for Civilian-Military Affairs have been Mary C. Yates (2007-09), J. Anthony Holmes (2009-12), and Christopher W. Dell (September 15, 2012, to the present). Proportionally, there are far fewer FSOs at a personal rank of Career Minister (a three-star equivalent) compared to Minister-Counselors (two-star equivalent) than there are three-star general or flag officers compared to two–stars. In this sense, a

Minister Counselor-ranked former ambassador is roughly equivalent to a three-star general or flag officer.

80. Technically speaking, the first AFRICOM Deputy to the Commander for Civil-Military Affairs was part of the U.S. European Command before the new Command's creation, so her Africa experience was available to one of AFRICOM's antecedents for a relatively brief period.

81. One source believed that the difference, beyond title, between the responsibilities of AFRICOM's Deputy to the Commander for Civil-Military Activities and the Southern Command's Civilian Deputy to the Commander were hard to distinguish. One concrete difference is that AFRICOM's Deputy supervised humanitarian and demining assistance, including the large HIV/AIDS in the military program, which the Southern Command's Civilian Deputy does not. The Southern Command's Civilian Deputy is also dual-hatted as the Foreign Policy Advisor, while this position is separated at AFRICOM. See *www.southcom.mil/aboutus/Pages/Ambassador-Carmen-Martinez.aspx*.

82. See *www.pacom.mil/organization/staff-directorates/j0/index.shtml*.

83. Ploch, "African Command."

84. Julian Barnes, "Defense Chief Urges Bigger Budget for State Department," *The Los Angeles Times*, November 27, 2007.

85. As quoted from Michael Reed, "Non-DOD Agencies of U.S. Africa Command," AFRICOM J-7, presentation, August 2012.

86. Congressional Research Service (CRS) Specialist in African Affairs Lauren Ploch Blanchard, in written comments to author, December 2012.

87. Reed, p. 8.

88. From September 15, 2011, State Africa Bureau phone list, unclassified. It is important to note that the number of FSOs and civil servants working on African policy issues at the DoS is higher than given here because there are a number of officials in function-

al bureaus of the Department who are also primarily responsible for Africa, as well as one office in the Bureau of Intelligence and Research dedicated exclusively to Africa. There are also a significant number of officials in the Bureau of Near Eastern Affairs who cover North Africa from Morocco to Egypt. In total, the author estimates, these other offices add anywhere from 50-100 officers covering African affairs at State. These figures also do not include the staffing levels of DoS personnel at U.S. Embassies in Africa or USAID personnel implementing our foreign aid programs in Africa.

89. Ploch, "African Command."

90. Ham, "Posture Statement of U.S. Africa Command." Note: Most Africa Contingency Operations Training and Assistance programs are carried out by contractors working for the DoS, not military personnel, who do occasionally serve as mentors in support of DoS programs.

91. Hooper, p. 10.

92. Thomas-Jensen, Winter 2008.

93. Ortiz, p. 8.

94. In fact, many critics of AFRICOM within the DoS and USAID are likely resigned to the fact that the Command, which is well funded, has chosen to carry out security-related development work.

95. Kate Almquist, "Africa Doesn't Need the Pentagon's Charity: Why I'm Grumpy about DOD's Development Programs in Africa," Washington, DC: Center for Global Development, August 29, 2012, available from *www.cgdev.org/content/article/detail/1426446/*.

96. Early in the Command's brief history, AFRICOM's most senior USAID officer was one of two Deputies in the J-5 responsible for programs. That officer left the Command, and his position was filled by a retired Navy rear admiral. In late 2010, another Senior Foreign Service USAID officer arrived at the Command as Senior Development Advisor, working directly for the Commander.

97. One congressional source indicated that Combined Joint Task Force-Horn of Africa (CJT-HOA) often used the broad rubric of "winning hearts and minds" to justify its civil affairs projects, but that their link to security has sometimes been tenuous.

98. Ploch, "AFRICOM: Rationales, Roles, and Progress on the Eve of Operations."

99. Almquist, "Africa Doesn't Need the Pentagon's Charity."

100. Allison Burket, "AFRICOM on the Horn of Africa: The Military's Fumbling Humanitarian Foot Forward," June, 9, 2010, available from *www.afjn.org/focus-campaigns/militarization-us-afr ica-policy/105-commentary/830-africom-on-the-horn-of-africa-the-mil itarys-fumbling-humanitarian-foot-forward.html*. See also "DOD Needs to Determine the Future of its Horn of Africa Task Force," GAO-1-504, April 2010.

101. Burket.

102. *Ibid.*

103. *Ibid.*

104. One senior AFRICOM official with whom the author spoke stated that U.S. Ambassadors must approve all AFRICOM projects in their countries. This does not diminish the author's recommendation that USAID and State should have the lead within a collaborative, multiagency project selection process.

105. Olson and Anderson.

106. McFate.

107. When ambassadors are not present in-country, U.S. diplomatic missions abroad are headed by ad interim chiefs of mission, known as charges d'affaires a.i. Charges are typically the deputy chief of mission (DCM), but sometimes a senior diplomat coming from Washington or out of retirement on temporary duty. Thus, "Chief of Mission" refers to the legally empowered head of the diplomatic mission, usually the ambassador, but sometimes another diplomat in an acting capacity.

108. Of course, AFRICOM must also carry out *internal* coordination with the Office of the Secretary of Defense, Joint Staff, Defense Intelligence Agency (DIA), Africa Center for Strategic Studies (ACSS), and other entities within the DoD. The focus of discussion here, however, is with U.S. Government entities *outside* of the DoD family.

109. Olson and Anderson.

110. Based on the comments of an anonymous source in AFRICOM's J-5 made in 2010-11.

111. The author's opinion is not merely academic, because he has served both the Senior Advisor to the J-5 Director at AFRICOM and the Senior Diplomatic Advisor at ACSS, which works closely with the Command. The author thus brings a unique perspective on interagency relations with AFRICOM, albeit just one perspective.

112. Ploch, July 22, 2011.

113. Don Yamamoto, "AFRICOM: Promoting Partnership for Global Security in Africa." House Foreign Affairs Committee Subcommittee on Africa, Global Health, and Human Rights, Washington, DC, July 26, 2011, Testimony available from *www.state.gov/p/af/rls/rm/2011/169150.htm.*

114. "Chief of Mission" is a term used synonymously with "Ambassador," but it can also refer to the head of U.S. diplomatic missions, such as to the AU, or to the Charge d'Affaires, typically the DCM, who is statutorily placed in charge of an embassy or other diplomatic mission in the absence of an ambassador. Quote is from "Commander's Intent." See Carter Ham, "Commander's Intent," Kelley Barracks, Stuttgart, Germany, August 2011.

115. Dennis R. Penn, "Africa Command and the Militarization of U.S. Foreign Policy," Carlisle, PA: U.S. Army War College Research Project, March 10, 2008.

116. The author learned of this effort while at AFRICOM. Assistant Secretary of State Johnnie Carson granted the author per-

mission to use this example during a one-on-one conversation on November 9, 2012.

117. The author has seen no evidence in the press that either Commander has ever veered off-message in terms of *policy* statements. One source asserted, however, that there had been concern in some parts of the DoS about statements by General Ham asserting a link between AQIM and Boko Haram. Even if General Ham had made such statements, however, they likely reflected his informed professional judgment of a state of play based on intelligence sources, rather than a statement of U.S. policy per se.

118. Testimony before the House Foreign Affairs Committee Subcommittee on Africa, Global Health, and Human Rights, July 26, 2011.

119. Yamamoto.

120. DoD launched Operation ENDURING FREEDOM — TRANS-SAHEL (OEF-TS) in 2007 to support Trans-Sahara Counter-Terrorism Partnership (TSCTP) programming.

121. Yamamoto.

122. GAO-10-794, July 2010.

123. Joe Quartararo, Sr., *et al.*, "Libya's Operation Odyssey Dawn, Command and Control," *Prism*, Vol. 3, No. 2, June 2012.

124. Ironically, several military officers from different branches of the armed services confided to the author that they experienced their own (likely more modest) bureaucratic culture shock of coming to a joint command and having to learn how to be effective in a joint staff environment and to understand the vernacular of other branches.

125. Olson and Anderson.

126. The "Regional Engagement Plans" in Table 4 have been replaced by Subordinate Campaign Plans. However, the table is still useful in terms of showing the linkage to non-DoD plans, most notably the Mission Strategic Resource Plans (MSRPs).

127. The author led an effort in 2010 in the Command's J-5 Directorate to craft the first model country work plan and develop an annual calendar for the preparation of these plans tied to DoD annual planning, assessments, and budgeting cycles.

128. Olson and Anderson.

129. Per author's conversation with senior J-5 AFRICOM official, January 2, 2013.

130. Ortiz, p. 6.

131. Laura Stephens and Jose Arimateia da Cruz, "The US Africa Command (AFRICOM): Building Partnership or Neo-Colonialism of US-Africa Relations?" *Journal of Third World Studies*, Vol. 27, No. 2, 2010.

132. Robert G. Berschinski, *AFRICOM'S Dilemma: The "Global War on Terrorism," "Capacity Building," Humanitarianism, and the Future of U.S. Security Policy in Africa*, Carlisle, PA: Strategic Studies Institute, U.S. Army War College, November 2007.

133. One senior U.S. Government official told author that African criticism of the DoD proposal to place AFRICOM's headquarters in Africa was particularly intense at the time—and in part for "rhetoric for public consumption"—because the United States was under intense criticism at the time for its role in Iraq. The author also notes that France has maintained a number of bases in its former colonies since independence, although the number of these bases has fallen over time. (See also discussion below on French attitudes toward AFRICOM.)

134. Ever since the "Blackhawk Down" incident in Somalia in 1993 that led to 18 American soldiers dead and 73 wounded, U.S. policy in Africa has been to avoid "U.S. boots on the ground" in combat situations. See *en.wikipedia.org/wiki/Battle_of_Mogadishu_*.

135. El-Rayah Osman, "More than Good Intentions: AFRICOM, between American Ambition and African Suspicion," *Military Professional Intelligence Bulletin*, January 1, 2012.

136. "Actions Needed to Address Stakeholder Concerns, Improve Interagency Collaboration, and Determine Full Costs Associated with the U.S. Africa Command," GAO-09-181, Washington, DC: U.S. GAO, February 2009.

137. Ham, "Posture Statement of U.S. Africa Command."

138. Pham.

139. Ploch, "African Command."

140. Danielle Skinner, "Ambassador J. Anthony Holmes Shares Parting Thoughts at AFRICOM," September 14, 2012.

141. Jim Garamone, "Official: U.S. DOD Seeks 'Small Footprint' in Africa," American Forces Press Service, October 15, 2012.

142. Another caveat in this admittedly unscientific anecdote is that it is not always clear whether a given source is really African, U.S., or a non-African third country opponent of AFRICOM.

143. "America in Africa: A Light Footprint. The Pentagon's Unusual African Arm," *The Economist*, April 14, 2011, available from *www.economist.com/node/18561821/*.

144. Whitlock.

145. Terje Ostebo, "Islamic Militancy in Africa," ACSS Africa Security Brief No. 23, November 2012, p. 2.

146. A senior AFRICOM official told the author in January 2013 that the Command had both counterterrorism and security cooperation missions (with the latter supporting counterterrorism as well as other policy goals). This official felt that the Command had "perhaps moved too far towards counterterrorism, but was moving back toward greater emphasis on security cooperation."

147. Sam Raphael and Doug Stokes, "Globalizing West African Oil: US 'Energy Security' and the Global Economy," *International Affairs*, Vol. 87, No. 4, 2011, p. 904.

148. See section on oil diplomacy in Brown, *Hidden Dragon, Crouching Lion.*

149. Ed Blanche, "Africom's Agenda Still Baffles Africa," *New African*, No. 481, February 2009.

150. Pham.

151. "How Dependent Are We on Foreign Oil," U.S. Energy Information Administration (EIA) Energy in Brief, July 13, 2012.

152. Brown, *Hidden Dragon, Crouching Lion.*

153. Based on ongoing research from multiple sources for David E. Brown, *African Oil and Natural Gas Exploration and Production: The Current State of Play and Longer-term Implications for the United States, China, and the Global Energy Market*, forthcoming academic paper.

154. The "Seven Sisters" was a term to describe the seven oil companies that formed the "Consortium for Iran" cartel and dominated the global petroleum industry from the mid-1940s to the 1970s. The group comprised Anglo-Persian Oil Company (now BP); Gulf Oil, Standard Oil of California (SoCal) and Texaco (now Chevron); Royal Dutch Shell; and Standard Oil of New Jersey (Esso) and Standard Oil Company of New York (Socony) (now ExxonMobil).

155. Raphael and Stokes, pp. 904, 917.

156. As quoted in "Misguided Intentions: Resisting AFRICOM," Captain Moussa Diop Mboup, Senegalese Army, Michael Mihalka, and Major Douglas Lathop, U.S. Army, ret., available from *www.army.mil//article/35036/Misguided_Intentions_Resisting_Africom/.*

157. Brown, *Hidden Dragon, Crouching Lion.*

158. *Ibid.*

159. *Ibid.*

160. Osman.

161. The Fashoda Incident or "Fashoda Crisis" (1898), was the climax of imperial territorial disputes between the British and France in Eastern Africa. A French expedition to Fashoda on the White Nile sought to gain control of the Nile River and thereby force Britain out of Egypt. The British held firm as Britain and France were on the verge of war. The incident ended in a diplomatic victory for the British and gave rise to the "Fashoda syndrome" in French foreign policy, or seeking to assert French influence in areas that might be becoming susceptible to British influence. Available from *en.wikipedia.org/wiki/Fashoda_Incident*.

162. Andrew Hansen, "The French Military in Africa," New York: Council on Foreign Relations, February 8, 2008.

163. C. Todd Lopez, "Dagger Brigade to 'Align' with AFRICOM in 2013," June 22, 2012, available from *www.army.mil/article/82376/Dagger_Brigade_to_align_with_AFRICOM_in_2013/*.

164. AFRICOM J-5 Synchronization Division Chief David Gaddis, e-mail to the author, January 8, 2013.

165. A senior J-5 official stressed to the author that these are "aligned" forces, not "assigned" forces, January 2, 2013, telephone conversation.

166. Paul McLeary, "U.S. Army Beefing Up Partnership With Special Forces in Africa," November 4, 2012, 2012.

167. "AFRICOM Expands Mission in Africa," available from *therealnews.com/t2/index.php?option=com_content&task=view&id=31&itemid=74&jumival=8346*.

168. Meles died on August 20, 2012, in a hospital in Europe. See *www.nytimes.com/2012/08/22/world/africa/meles-zenawi-ethiopian-leader-dies-at-57.html?_r=0*.

169. United States support for force generation for peacekeeping missions and in the provision of training and equipment to troop-contributing countries is the responsibility of the DoS, not DoD or AFRICOM. State's Africa, Political-Military, and Interna-

tional Organizations Bureaus share this responsibility, drawing on funding provided to the State Department by Congress.

170. The AU Mission in Somalia was created by the AU Peace and Security Council on January 19, 2007, with an initial 6-month mandate. On February 21, 2007, the UN Security Council approved the mission's mandate, which has been renewed every 6 months since then, available from *en.wikipedia.org/wiki/African_ Union_Mission_to_Somalia*. The UN-AU operation in Darfur was established on July 31, 2007, with the adoption of Security Council resolution 1769. See *www.un.org/en/peacekeeping/missions/unamid/*.

171. Consistent with U.S. law and policy, the DoS vets its assistance to foreign security forces, as well as certain DoD training programs, to ensure that recipients have not committed gross human rights abuses. When the vetting process uncovers credible information that an individual or unit has committed a gross violation of human rights, U.S. assistance is withheld. The obligation to vet DoS assistance and DoD-funded training programs for foreign security forces units is in section 620M (a.k.a., the Leahy Amendment) of the Foreign Assistance Act of 1961 [FAA]), as amended, and a comparable provision in the annual DoD Appropriations Act. While the State legislation applies to all "assistance" under the FAA and the Arms Export Control Act, the DoD law is specific to "training programs" funded under Defense Department Appropriations Acts, available from *www.humanrights. gov/2011/10/06/an-overview-of-the-leahy-vetting-process/*.

172. Skinner.

173. Mboup *et al.*

174. Ham, "Posture Statement of U.S. Africa Command."

175. Remarks by AFRICOM Commander General Carter Ham, made at AFRICOM Military and Media Symposium, September 7, 2012, in Garmisch, Germany.

176. "America in Africa: A Light Footprint," *The Economist*, April 14, 2011.

177. John Vandiver, "AFRICOM headquarters to Stay in Germany, Dempsey Says," *Stars and Stripes*, December 17, 2012.

178. Michael J. Mazarr, "The Risks of Ignoring Strategic Insolvency," *The Washington Quarterly*, Fall 2012 p. 8.

179. David Ignatius, "The Foreign Policy Debate We Should be Having," *The Washington Post*, October 19, 2012.

180. "Financial Summary Tables," *Department of Defense Budget for Fiscal Year 2013*, February 2012, p. 9.

181. Ploch, "African Command."

182. Mazarr, p. 14.

183. Ham, "Posture Statement of U.S. Africa Command."

184. See Craig Whitlock, "Contractors Run Spying Missions in Africa," and "U.S. Shares Fruit of Spy Missions," *The Washington Post*, June 14, 2012.

185. Based on January 2, 2013 e-mail communication between the author and AFRICOM senior official.